D0667436

The
Long-Drive
Bible

The
Long-Drive
Bible

HOW YOU CAN HIT THE BALL LONGER, STRAIGHTER, AND MORE CONSISTENTLY

SEAN FISTER AND MATTHEW RUDY

WILEY

John Wiley & Sons, Inc.

Copyright © 2008 by Sean Fister. All rights reserved

Published by John Wiley & Sons, Inc., Hoboken, New Jersey
Published simultaneously in Canada

Photographs © J. D. Cuban

Design and composition by Navta Associates, Inc.

For general information about our other products and services, please contact our Customer Care Department within the United States at (800) 762-2974, outside the United States at (317) 572-3993 or fax (317) 572-4002.

Wiley also publishes its books in a variety of electronic formats. Some content that appears in print may not be available in electronic books. For more information about Wiley products, visit our web site at www.wiley.com.

Library of Congress Cataloging-in-Publication Data:
Fister, Sean, date.
    The long-drive bible : how you can hit the ball longer, straighter, and more consistently / Sean Fister.
        p. cm.
    ISBN 978-0-470-11665-4 (cloth : alk. paper)
    1. Golf—Drive. I. Title.
    GV979.D74F57 2008
    796.352′3—dc22

                                                                                    2007035513

Printed in the United States of America

10 9 8 7 6 5 4 3 2 1

Contents

Foreword

I've been playing golf with Sean Fister for years—just two good old boys from Arkansas swinging hard and having fun. The funny thing is, when we first got started, I could hit it past him pretty easily. It'd crack me up, because he'd get so mad when I hit it by him by 10 or 20 yards.

One thing you learn pretty quickly when you meet Sean is that when he puts his mind to something, he gets it done—no matter what the obstacles are. I mean, this is a guy who's had some serious injuries to his back from all the pole-vaulting he did. He's not even supposed to be able to physically do what he's doing. And he's had people telling him every step of the way he wouldn't make it to the top. Those things just make him more determined to prove them wrong.

So when I hit it by him one time too many one summer, he went home and worked his tail off on getting better. And the next time we played, I'll be damned if Sean didn't hit it 30 yards by me on the first tee. Hey, anybody can get lucky and catch one solid, and he *is* a big dude. But I figured I'd show him who was in charge on the second hole, and I caught one real good there. Sure enough, Sean hit it by me again by 20 yards. At that point, I knew it was a good thing that I played a "complete" game of golf, because I wouldn't have made much money going head-to-head with him in long driving. He really is The Beast.

I have a ton of respect for Sean because he's worked his way to the top of long driving, but he's stayed the same good dude he's always been. He's a regular guy with an incredible talent. I've seen him around some of the most famous people in golf and sports, and I've seen him with the guys we hang out with in Little Rock, and he's the same guy. You can't say that about too many people.

If you want to hit the ball longer, listen to what Sean's got to say here. The talent he has comes naturally, but the work he put in to figure out how to get every yard out of his swing made him the hitter he is. He knows what works and what doesn't, and he can help you untangle all the complicated, contradictory swing advice that's out there. He can give you a shortcut to 20 more yards on your tee shots. It doesn't get much better than that, does it?

Grip it and rip it.

—JOHN DALY
*Winner of the 1991 PGA Championship and the 1995 British Open, and
11-time PGA Tour leader in driving distance*

INTRODUCTION

Nobody ever showed me how to hit a golf ball, or how to hit it far. I've spent thousands of hours figuring out for myself how to hold the club, how to stand, and how to hit the ball with one simple goal: kill it. I hit a lot of crooked shots and broke enough clubheads and shafts to fill up a tractor-trailer. I pissed off more than a few people along the way, too. But I have a room full of trophies—including three for winning the World Long-Drive Championship—in a house paid for with the money I made doing what I do best. When I hit it solid, I've never been beat.

It took me twenty years to put it all together, but everything I've learned—from technique to training to the emotional and mental game you have to play to succeed on the big stage—is in this book. It's not designed to be a guide on how to make it as a professional long driver (hey, I want to win a few more titles before I quit). It's for the average guy out there who'd like to get 10 or 20 more yards on his tee shot and win some more money in his weekend game. I'm not exaggerating when I say that this is the first book to offer this kind of help. I know, because I would have loved to have the help when I was learning, and I looked everywhere for it. I had to do it the hard way, sorting through hundreds of tips and techniques, separating what works from what doesn't, and proving it out by hitting more balls than most people think is possible. (You can hit a thousand balls in a day. I've done it. It takes seven hours.)

I dug it out, and now you don't have to.

In chapter 1 of this book, I'll give you an inside look at the sport of long driving and how we do what we do. I think it'll give you a new appreciation not just for the strength it takes to hit a 390-yard tee shot, but also for the technique and focus. Next, I'll tell you how I dug my long-drive secrets out of the dirt—how I condensed hundreds of swing thoughts and tips into ten core commandments that I keep with me in a little black book I carry to every tournament.

In chapter 3, we'll go over those commandments one by one, from how high to tee the ball to get the best launch angle to how to smoke it straight when you absolutely need to. Chapter 4 is devoted to curing the biggest problem most amateur players face: the slice. I have two pages in my little black book devoted to antislice tips, and I'll share the best ones with you.

In chapter 5, we'll go over the best strategies to use off the tee to get the most out of every shot you hit. Chapter 6 is all about the stretching and the strength-training exercises I do to get ready for the World Championship, and the focusing routines I developed when I was a world-class pole-vaulter in college.

Technology has more impact on your tee shot than on any other shot you hit during a round of golf. Finding the right shaft-clubhead combination is the difference between finishing first and fifteenth at the World Championship, and it's the difference between a mediocre tee shot and a real bomb when you play.

Chapter 7 will show you how to get the most out of your equipment. In chapter 8 I'll give you some drills you can practice at the range to groove your new swing technique.

I'm the first one to say that I'm thankful for everything the sport of long driving has given me. But that doesn't mean the system we have is perfect. Everybody who knows me knows I've got strong opinions and I'm not afraid to express them. Our sport could be bigger and get a lot more exposure, and the last chapter lists some of the things I'd do to bring long driving to more fans and make it more fair for the guys competing.

One more thing before we get out there and beat some balls. The next time you're up late, watching one of those infomercials on the Golf Channel from some guy who tells you he's the world record holder for hitting it long, keep this in mind: there might be five or six guys in the world who can consistently carry the ball 350 yards. I'm one of them, and I know all the rest of them personally. If anybody else wants to prove he belongs in that group, let me make this challenge right here, right now. Come on out to Little Rock and we'll go down to the Arkansas River. It's 360 yards across. I know I can hit it over. I've done it. We'll have ourselves a competition. If you can make it across, we'll back it up five steps and try it again. The last guy to clear the river wins. And bring your checkbook.

When we're done here, I'm not saying you'll be able to fly it over my river. But you'll be able to carry some of the hazards at your course that were a little too long for you before. Trust me when I tell you there's nothing better than catching one solid and hearing your buddies say, "Man, you got all of that one."

Let's hit it.

1

INSIDE THE BELLY
OF THE BEAST:
BEHIND THE SCENES
AT THE WORLD LONG-DRIVE
CHAMPIONSHIP

There's nothing like standing there on the tee in final round of the World Long-Drive Championship, under the lights, with the grid stretching out in front of you in the Nevada desert, glowing green in the middle of all that sand. Four thousand people are jammed into the grandstand 20 feet behind you, but you can't hear them. That's the thing that tightens your throat the most—how silent it gets when you're set up over your shot, trying to hit a big, big ball to win the title you've spent almost every waking moment of the year preparing for. It can make a 50-yard-wide grid look like a two-lane road. Those portable stadium lights feel like they're all pointed right at you.

In the final round, every guy there can take it deep, with club-head speed 25 miles per hour faster than the longest players on the PGA Tour can generate—fast enough to hit a golf ball through a three-quarter-inch-thick piece of plywood. Those six guys are the top of a long-drive pyramid that started with 14,000 local qualifiers and finishes in one of sports' biggest pressure cookers. Since the World Championship started in 1995, I've made the final round seven times, and I've won 'em—and lost 'em—every way you can do it.

In 2001, I hit what's been called the most clutch shot in the history of the sport, a 376-yard drive on my last ball in the final round to win my second world title. But sometimes it goes the other way, too. In 2000, I was swinging faster and hitting it harder than anybody in Nevada, but I couldn't keep it on the grid, and I didn't get through the semifinals. In the 1997 final round, I hit one 406 yards, right down the middle of the grid, but my ball rolled into a bunker nobody thought was in play. Jason Zuback hit it 412 just to the side of the same bunker and beat me.

Of all the guys who have a dream that they can someday say they're the biggest hitter in golf, only 128 of them make it to Mesquite, Nevada, to take their shot at getting on ESPN under those lights. The championship is organized in a modified round-robin format. We get divided into eight groups of sixteen with two heats each, and the only way to guarantee that you'll move forward is to finish in the top two of your heat. You get six balls in each round to prove you deserve to go to the next round. Get a bad draw, with two guys who are just cranking it? Too bad. Not swinging your best the first day of the event? You don't get any mulligans, and there's no next week. You're going home, no matter what your name is.

What you *can* control is hitting your best shot and making other guys beat you. Look at everybody hitting on the range, and you're not going to pick me to win. But you can't see what's in a guy's gut or in his heart. When I won in 2005, there were a lot of guys who could flat kill it who didn't get to the finals. It's not about the guy who can hit it the longest. It's about the guy who can manage his emotions, hit it solid, and handle everybody watching him.

I've been in this sport twenty years, and I've seen funny things happen to guys who looked like they were cut out of stone. I've watched guys who hit it 390 in the first round of qualifying on Thursday but couldn't tee it up in the quarterfinals because their hands were shaking so much. Just like the PGA Tour or the NBA, at this level it's not all about who has the most physical skill or strength. You've got to be an exceptional hitter of the golf ball to get yourself in position to win a World Long-Drive Championship, but the true test is what goes on in your head, not with your muscles or your golf swing.

I've seen it happen a hundred times. There's a core group of four or five guys who are the favorites, year after year, guys who have proven themselves time and again. We show up expecting to make the final group of six. And every year there's some phenomenal guy who's supposed to hit it out of sight and beat everybody. But it's always the same guys who advance. It's been that way for twenty years. Why is that?

Almost every other guy in the sport is beat before he even hits his first ball. It's easy to see why. When you get to the practice range at the World Championship, you see twenty or thirty big, muscular guys wailing away. You hear all the whispering about who did what in practice or in the qualifying—how this guy hit it 400 yards, or that guy is really killing it. You see Zuback, with his five world titles, or Viktor Johansson, the 2000 champion, who's 6 foot 6 and 280 pounds. It's like that scene in the movie *Hoosiers* when the kids from Hickory are watching the team from South Bend Central warm up before the state championship game. Some guys need Gene Hackman to come by and remind them that the grid is 55 yards wide for everybody, not just the stars.

Wondering whether you belong is a huge hurdle for a lot of guys, because you just never know. If you aren't mentally strong, you can't walk down the driving range without blowing all your confidence. You see a new shaft or a new head, and you think a guy has something you don't, and there's a little doubt there. It happened to me early in my career, and I learned the hard way that I needed to trust my preparation, do my thing, and hit my ball. The guys who haven't figured that out yet? They're donators. They're the ones who sign on for the championship year after year with no chance to win—like all those amateurs who spend $10,000 to enter the World Series of Poker. It's dead money. Those entry fees have been paying part of my winner's checks.

I'll be on the practice range getting ready on Tuesday morning of championship week and I'll see a new guy out there, just killing it. You can tell he's feeling good about himself by the way he's posing after every shot, kind of checking out of the corner of his eye to see if anybody's watching. After 30 or 40 shots, he puts his driver away and takes a walk down the range to see what he's up against—to see who's going to finish second. He'll walk behind Dave Gureckis, who really smokes it in practice, and just turn dead pale. Then he goes back to his bag all flustered and starts looking for a new driver—something to help him find the 20 more yards he knows he's going to need. When he starts hitting it again, he's lunging at it, overswinging and getting out of sync.

Or worse yet, he'll go over to one of the equipment reps working the range and ask for a lighter shaft—the day before the event! The guy has been getting ready for four months, and he gets to Mesquite and changes everything he's doing. Swing, setup, all of it. It's crazy. He's been practicing by himself for four months, admiring the big balls he hits on his range at home, but when it comes time to do it with the lights on, that's a different beast. I'm telling you, it takes a lot of self-confidence to be able to block that out and just do your thing.

The entire week of the championship, I've got a thousand-yard stare on, concentrating on what I've got going on in front of me—to the point that friends walk by and say hello and I don't even hear them. It's not me being an asshole. It's focus. Hey, this isn't camp or some kind of retreat or vacation. It blows my mind to see guys treat it as if it is, because winning can change your life. I'm not saying I've never stayed out a little too late the night before a tournament, but when I saw how much money I could make, I got real serious about it.

The reality of our sport is that the pool of talent is very wide in terms of guys who have the ability to hit the ball far, but the payout is only there for a select few who can kill it, but also have the charisma to be appealing to corporate America. It costs me $500 to enter the World Championship. Add another $3,000 in expenses for the week there. Come in third, and after taxes I might break even. Might. There are three or four of us making six figures as long drivers. The key is to be able to capitalize when you win the World Championship and show the world what you can do, because you aren't going to make your nut just from the prize money.

The 2001 event is what made it for me. When I won the 1995 title, I was pretty much unknown, and the sport hadn't gotten a lot of exposure on ESPN yet. By 2001, Zuback had drawn a ton of attention, winning four straight titles and getting on the cover of *Golf Digest*. The first-prize check had moved up to $80,000, from the $30,000 it was in 1995.

I sure picked the right year to hit the shot of my life.

The final group set up almost as if it was planned for television. Zuback hit the longest ball of all the semifinalists, at 378, and Brian Pavlet had been hitting it great all week. Zuback came up second and had what was for him a bad set. He hit it 353, seven yards behind Pat Dempsey, who had come out first. Pavlet crushed his second ball 373 to take the lead, then came back to the practice range after he finished to let me know I was going to have to bring it. He walked behind me as I was hitting balls and started snapping tees to get my attention. He said, "You better hit it hard."

I drew the last slot of the six, so I knew exactly what I had to do. The left side of the grid was firm, where they'd been driving some maintenance carts through during the week. I got up and aimed down that side but hooked the first two out of bounds. I aimed a little more right on the third one and lost it to the right. I didn't quite catch the fourth one, but at least got it into play at 361. On my fifth ball, I blocked another out of bounds to the right.

The crowd was going nuts, howling for me to catch my last ball solid. But when I stepped up behind the ball to start my routine, they went completely quiet. I looked over and saw people patting Pavlet on the back. I saw another guy lean over to Brian and say to him, "There's no way." Honestly, that really pissed me off. I knew Brian was watching to see if I was going to take his first world title away from him and crossing his fingers. There's no way? I wanted so badly to show them there *was* a way, and I was going to lay it on them right there.

I went through my complete focusing routine (which I'll tell you more about in chapter 6), took a deep breath, and let it go. At impact, I knew I hit it hard enough. But I've been in enough of these championships to know that the ball can hit soft and check up, even if you carry it deep. The grid is like a checkerboard. It isn't consistent, like the lane at a bowling alley. My ball landed at 357 and released and rolled out past 373. When I saw it roll past Brian's mark, I just went nuts, high-fiving people in the stands and generally just losing my mind. I had hit it 376 on the last ball, when the temperature was dropping, with no tailwind. It was the greatest shot of my life, at the biggest moment, on the last ball of the entire championship. That's going to be tough to top, even if I stay in the sport another ten years.

Now that I'm one of the "old guys" out there, I'm sure the younger guys roll their eyes when I start talking about how different the World Championship is now compared to when I got started. But it's true. Back in the early 1990s, when it was the National Championship, not the World Championship, you had forty or fifty guys out there competing. There were fifteen or twenty really tight guys and then another twenty or so on the fringe, and that was the sport, period. It was very hard to break into that clique, and it didn't happen for me until 1995. You used to want to see other guys do well, almost because there wasn't enough money in it to get really upset about.

And the scene surrounding the championship? It's incredible how much that's changed. When I started competing, there might have been a hundred people in the gallery—and 90 percent of them were competitors who had been eliminated, the rest being family members. There weren't enough to fill even a small set of stands behind the tee. We held the event at some nice places, but it was probably more of a nuisance to the resorts that hosted it than anything else. Evan "Big Cat" Williams was the big attraction then, and what he was doing—fifty or so exhibitions a year—was considered the ultimate. When Art Sellinger got involved and basically bought the sport, in the early 1990s, things got much more organized. When I won in 1995, I think there were 2,500 entrants in the field. In 2001, there were 13,000. The main growth of the sport has come from the competitors—the number of guys who are chasing the dream—but fan attention has grown, too. More than 3,000 people were in the stands for the 2006 final round.

The finals were out in Mesquite for the first time in 1997, but they hadn't quite figured it all out yet. They put us on the actual first hole of the Casablanca Golf Club, hitting from the back tee, 415 yards from the green. I walked the grid with Art Sellinger early in the week, and we had a hellacious tailwind. I told him that somebody was going to hit the ball into the middle of that bunker in the finals and get screwed. Sure enough, I carried it 386 in the final round and landed it right in the middle of that trap. Zuback hit his three or four yards right of mine, missed the trap, and rolled it up onto the green to beat me. After that happened, they moved it across town to the driving range at the Palms, the setup you see now on ESPN every year.

Winning on the last ball in 2001 got me a tremendous amount of attention. ESPN made it an ESPN Classic episode, and it must have run fifty or sixty times. I got out there and made some good sponsorship deals—people want to be around people who are good at something. In 1997, I saw an ad for Dunlop, and I wanted to get balls for free, so I wrote a letter to the president of the company asking him if he wanted to have the longest driver in America hit his golf ball. I told him I'd earn the money first. I'd get on ESPN during the World Championship, and I'd work my ass off to get his brand as much exposure as possible. I did get on television at the championship, and I was in an instruction spread in *Golf Tips* magazine, so Dunlop gave me a contract for $25,000. I started showing up at tournaments with a lot of logos all over my shirt, and there was a quite a bit of sniping that went with that.

One year, I went to the PGA Merchandise Show, and I came to find out that two fringe long drivers had gone to all my sponsors and told them they were friends of mine and wanted deals, too. Of course, I had no idea who they were. That was just the start of all the jealousy and backstabbing that goes on. But when the top guys started making some money at this sport, a lot of things changed.

When I won my title in 2001, I basically took it away from Pavlet on that last big drive—and it would have been his first world championship. I know he was just devastated and felt like he had missed his big chance. We had been good friends for five or six years before that, rooming together on the road and everything. But after 2001, we drifted apart, and he stopped returning my calls. We exchange hugs and hellos at the World Championship, but that's about it. They joke about it being lonely at the top, but it's true. Zuback might be the only other guy who knows how that feels.

There are so many misconceptions about what this sport is like and what winning the World Championship does for you. Winning by itself doesn't change your life. You have to be marketable, too. You have to be able to carry a conversation with a corporate executive. You have to be able to talk to his customers. You have to know when to talk and when to be quiet. You have to know when to talk business and when not to.

Zuback and I get paid more than anybody else, without a doubt, as far as active competitors go. There might be three or four guys on the tier right below who make a decent living. Below that are guys who make some money but still need to have a day job. The level below that, they're making no money at this. We don't turn anybody away, that's for sure. It's grassroots. If you can swing the club 150 miles per hour, it doesn't matter what you look like. But if the wrong guy catches one and wins, that's going to back the sport up a little bit because he doesn't know what to do with it. We've already got the image of a bunch of gorillas who swing hard but don't know how to play real golf. All we need is some guy in a yellow tank top and spandex shorts winning a world title to send it right over the edge. That's not exactly going to grow the sport.

Now, expanding the World Championship to 15,000 people instead of 50 has brought some big benefits, especially for me. It means more entry fee money and more attention from the media. That certainly makes my sponsors happy. But the drawback is that there are a lot of young, strong guys who are getting interested in what I have.

You used to be able to be conservative early in the competition and kind of work your way into it. I've always broken my six balls into two groups of three; I'm conservative on the first three and aggressive on the second three, once I have a qualifier on the grid. But when more guys got into the sport, the early rounds started getting filled with these giant guys you don't know anything about. It's too risky to go through an early round now expecting to coast. One of those monsters could get lucky and catch one and send you home. I know I have to keep one "scary ball" in reserve if I need it, because there's a chance somebody could pop one and take me out.

The improvements in equipment certainly have been great for the average guy playing his weekend game, for sure. It's so much easier to hit the ball than it used to be, with big-headed drivers and balls that don't spin as much. And the longest drivers in the sport are hitting it longer than ever. But the flip side is that the big, forgiving drivers give every half-talented guy a puncher's chance, especially early in the event. They've even widened the grid from 40 yards to 55 to encourage this whole gunslinger mentality. It's a testament to Zuback that he's been able to win five titles, because he has to prove himself every year, every round, and fight his way through a forest of 6-foot-6 guys built like superheroes, just like I do.

You can imagine what happens when you have a group of 128 big, strong guys who swing a club as hard as possible getting together. There's a tremendous amount of ego and testosterone overflowing. That applies to everything from the way a guy walks up and down the practice range to the way he wears a skintight shirt to show off his muscles. Guys are trying to use intimidation to gain an advantage, even if it's a small one. I've definitely had people tell me I look intimidating. Maybe it's because I don't always trim my goatee just right. I'm known as an opinionated guy, and that's also given me problems over the years (and I'm sure saying stuff like this in this book won't help).

The funny thing about all that ego and testosterone is that it changes the dynamic of the competition. When you're playing golf against an opponent, deep down you're hoping he makes a mistake so you can win. I know that's what I'm thinking when my buddy Doug is standing over a birdie putt back home. But in long driving, you're hoping the guy who's going against you in the finals absolutely nuts it and hits his career drive. Because if he doesn't, and you get up there and beat him, he's going to remind you of that for the rest of your life—to the point that your win seems almost tainted.

Believe me, I know how crazy that sounds. But I'll be the first to admit that my win in 2001 was the most satisfying, because the last ball I hit was as hard as I could hit one, and I heard the first four finalists say in their interviews that they had hit it with all they had. That meant that my best was better than their best. And when I've hit my best shot, I've never been beat.

Does that make me cocky? Probably. But I think it's also what gives me my edge. I want to win so badly and I want to beat those guys so much that I'm basically willing myself to do it. If I'm going up against a guy who's adjusting his shirt so it looks good on television or is preoccupied with the color of the shaft on his driver, he's got no chance.

Everybody wants the attention. Long driving isn't any different from Ultimate Fighting or even NBA basketball in that respect.

When I first started, it was about the recognition, sure, but it was also about the money. I was trying to make this my job. Now that I've been successful, I've got contracts that pay me enough that it's only about winning. I don't worry as much about the money. I want more hardware. And to leave a legacy.

2

THE GENESIS OF THE
LONG-DRIVE BIBLE

You don't have to flip to the pictures in the next chapter to figure out that I've got a homemade golf swing. I'll tell you that straight up right here. But I'm proud of that, and I'm proud of the fact that I figured out how to hit it long enough and straight enough to stay at the elite level of long driving for twenty years.

It's hard to believe, but I never really thought about hitting a golf ball until I was in my early twenties. To be honest, I didn't think of golf as a real sport before then, and I didn't know something like long driving even existed.

The way I figured out how to hit it far was more hardheaded determination than anything else. You might look at me and think that you don't have much in common with a guy who's 6 foot 5, 250 pounds, and can hit a ball 400 yards. That's not exactly true. Whenever somebody refers to me as an athlete, I laugh a little bit. Because for the longest time, I was as far away from an athlete as you could be.

I grew up in small town in southern Missouri called Poplar Bluff, the third of four brothers. Kevin, Dan, and Corby were all great athletes. My older brothers, Kevin and Dan, were tough and strong, and my younger brother, Corby, got scholarship offers for football and baseball and was an outfielder in the Atlanta Braves organization. The talent probably came from my dad. He was a pitcher in the St. Louis Cardinals farm system, and Stan Musial was quoted as saying, "Rogers Fister could throw a strawberry through a battleship." My dad could also hit a golf ball 400 yards—with a persimmon driver.

If you were hanging around Poplar Bluff in the late 1970s, you knew all about the Fister boys. My two older brothers were the toughest guys in our town by far, and they caused more than their share of trouble. I fought them every day. They used to chase me off the school bus, to the point where the driver would hang the door a little on them to give me a running start. As the smaller, weaker kid, I hated every minute of it, but there's no doubt I got my competitiveness from them. It didn't matter if it was home-run derby in the yard or checkers in the living room, I wanted to beat them so badly I can't even describe it.

I had a big growth spurt between eighth and ninth grade, and I was a skinny, uncoordinated string bean. In ninth grade I tried out for football and got cut because they said I was too small. I tried out for baseball and got cut. I tried out for basketball and got cut. I wanted to be an athlete, but I couldn't find anything that they'd let me do. I ended up on the track team because it was the only team that didn't get rid of anybody. I was slow and weak, so I became the third-string pole-vaulter. In tenth grade, eighth graders were beating me pretty easily. You can call me cocky now—you need confidence to do what I do—but I certainly wasn't back then, when I couldn't clear nine feet if you gave me a ladder.

What I had going for me was the same thing that has won me three world championships in long driving. I was willing to stay out there and practice at it until I got better, even if I didn't have anybody showing me the right way to do it. The summer before my junior year, I made some uprights in my backyard out of some extra 2-by-2 pieces of wood and put nails in the boards every two inches, just like the pit at school. I went out there every day for three months and pole-vaulted in the yard, going over the bar and landing and rolling on the grass. When I came back to school in the fall, I could jump 12 feet, and by the end of my senior year I was jumping 13'8"—which broke the school record at Poplar Bluff by a foot. I held that record for more than twenty years. I won the conference and district championships that year, and later on, Bill Caputo, my coach, called me the greatest success story in the history of the school, because I had done so much with so little. That meant a lot, because Coach Caputo was like a father to me in high school.

When I graduated from high school, I was 6 foot 3, 150 pounds—and not really interested in going to school anymore. There wasn't much money—my dad had left when I was seven, and my mom, Ann, was doing the best she could on her own with seven of us kids. I was getting ready to join the Marines when my high school coach called and said he had gotten a letter from Park College in Kansas City, offering me a scholarship. When I wasn't getting into trouble, I was jumping pretty high—fifth in the nation for NAIA after my freshman year. I broke both my feet in a fall my sophomore year, but my junior year I jumped just under 16 feet (which is still the school record, twenty-six years later).

My dream was to pole-vault in the Olympics, so I figured I needed to get someplace warm, where I could vault all year. Coach Mike Bozeman ran the field events at the University of Florida, and he was tremendously well respected as a vaulting coach. I drove down to Gainesville after my junior year, without any money

or any scholarship. I walked into Coach Bozeman's office, and
before I even said a word he told me he had requested my files
from Park, and if he had known about my disciplinary problems I
wouldn't have been there. The bottom line was, I was down to my
last chance. I grew up without my dad, so I was always looking to
coaches to fill that void. I couldn't have picked a better role model
than Coach Bozeman. He and I ended up like father and son, and
there's no doubt I wouldn't be where I am without him.

I got a room in the athletic dorm at Florida, but I didn't have any
money for a food plan. The guys on the track team brought me extra
food from the cafeteria, and I got a job pumping gas to make some
money. I started out as the seventh vaulter on the team, but by the
end of the year I was one of the better vaulters in the nation, and
one of the few people to walk on and earn a scholarship in less than
a year. I had a realistic chance to qualify for the 1984 Olympics.

Coach Bozeman took a job as the head track coach at Virginia
Military Institute after my senior year, and he got me a job there
so I could keep training with him. I was there six months working
hard and getting better, but then I broke my back on a bad vault. I
had gotten a lot stronger when I was at Florida, and I was a pretty
big guy at that point. My size was a problem because I started
breaking a lot of poles. When you break poles you get hurt. The
broken back was just the latest in a long line of injuries: I broke my
right foot eight times and my left four times, cracked my skull on
the edge of the pit on a bad vault once, and another time almost
lost my left thumb. I also severed the trapezius muscle at the base
of my head and tore cartilage in both knees.

I didn't have any health insurance, and I was all by myself in a
freezing one-room garage apartment. I was living off a deer leg a
guy gave me. I'd take it out of the freezer and run some hot water

over it, then shave off some meat and fry it in a pan. I was trying to work construction despite the back injury, and my boss took pity on me and told me he'd pay for me to see a doctor. I had a crack in my vertebrae. It would heal, but I was done vaulting, the doctor said. So I got in my car at midnight that night and drove straight back to Missouri. The Olympics weren't going to happen for me.

My first real job after school was working construction, installing utility pipes. My specialty was working the jackhammer, and after a summer of that I was really strong. They're still telling the story about the day when I broke up a half-mile stretch of asphalt all by myself. Drag a 75-pound jackhammer up and down the blacktop in the middle of an Arkansas summer and you'll get an idea of what that was like. It was great motivation to find something else to do.

The muscles I built from training and the jackhammer had the side benefit of giving me a lot of bat speed. After I moved down to Little Rock to take a job at Dillard's department store, I played on the company softball team. I could hit a softball harder and farther than anyone I knew—I mean, literally out of sight. After watching a few of those shots, Mike Dillard, the son of the founder, started calling me the Beast. The nickname stuck.

My golf career really started by accident. My brother Corby played a little bit, and he took me out to hit a round just for laughs. I shot a million and drove a couple of par-4s, but I didn't really know what that meant. I was out there swinging as hard as I could, just like I did on the softball field. That summer, I drove every par-4 at the Poplar Bluff municipal golf course. I was shooting 100, but it didn't matter to me. I was having a good time swinging out of my shoes. I can still remember hitting the longest drive of my life back then, with a steel-shafted, persimmon-headed driver. I hit it three feet past the flag on a 512-yard par-5 at Rebsamen Golf Course in Little Rock, with the help of a 40-mile-per-hour tailwind and a hardpan fairway. Made the putt, too.

The head pro at the Poplar Bluff course was a man by the name of Buddy Godwin. He's still kind of the golf guru of the area—a real traditionalist, too. He had been hearing all the stories about how far I was hitting the ball, and I'm sure he was a little tired of it. He was sitting there one Saturday reading the paper, and he saw a story about a local qualifying contest for the 1989 National Long-Drive Championship. He called me over and said, "I've been hearing about how far you hit it. If you're so long, why don't you go up there and try it out against the big boys? Those guys can really hit it."

If you tell me I can't do something, I'll do everything I can to prove you wrong, and I was going to show Buddy Godwin. I made a few calls, paid my entry fee, and went up to St. Louis. I had my regular off-the-rack 43-inch driver out of my bag. The rest of the guys there had 55- or 60-inch clubs, custom made. I ended up taking sixth place, and the top five made it to the district tournament. About two weeks before the district, I got a phone call. One guy had to go to college, and as the first alternate, I was in. I got myself a 46-inch club and practiced a little bit with that. At the districts, I flew one 338 yards, and nobody beat it. That got me into the National Championship down in Freeport, Bahamas.

I got down to the Bahamas and found a different world. The range was full of guys who could hit it 350 yards, and I was just one of them. I didn't know anybody, and I didn't even really know what I was supposed to be doing. Another long driver, "Big Wave" Dave Menary, came over and started talking to me and told me he liked how I hit the ball. I was desperately trying to fit in, and Dave made me feel like I belonged. I didn't advance in the tournament, but it was a learning experience. I saw that I could physically do what the guys who were winning could do, and I figured that if I applied myself to getting better at hitting long drives like I did to pole-vaulting, I could win myself a title.

When I got back to Poplar Bluff, I tried to find somebody who could teach me. The problem is, there are no experts on long driving. What does it say that the guy who has helped me the most isn't a golf pro? Coach Bozeman can't hit a golf ball very far; hell, he couldn't pole-vault 17 feet either, but he taught me how to do that. And what he taught me about concentrating intensely during competition has been the reason I've done as well as I have in long driving. But golf instruction? The actual mechanics of the golf swing? I figured out pretty quickly I was going to have to dig it out of the ground myself.

I started with one teacher, and he told me I should swing 85 percent and just try to hit it solid. That's really all he had for me—and it wasn't even swing advice. Hitting it solid to get it in the grid is strategy advice, and I already had that part down. Sam Snead saw me hitting balls and took me aside for some instruction. Bob Toski gave me a lesson. So did Jimmy Ballard. Marshal Smith, from Miami, Oklahoma, gave me some simple things that helped. All of those guys gave me something to work on—some position to try to get myself into—but there was never a "eureka" moment. They all told me to slow this down or slow that down. The problem is, I can't slow anything down. In this line of work, if you slow down, you get beat. It's so hard to find help with technique, because it's all happening so fast. It's like taking your NASCAR car to Sears and asking the guy there to fix it with the tools he has in the shop.

I was frustrated as hell, because I wasn't winning anything. In early 1995, I decided to go back to the summer I spent vaulting over the 2-by-2s in my yard. My mind-set has always been that I'm not afraid to work hard. If determination and persistence will get me there, I'll get there. When you work hard, you get a feeling of entitlement, that you deserve whatever you get. That feeling gives you a confidence that's almost impossible to shake. I knew that feeling, and I was going to get it again.

I never threw away any of my *Golf Digest* magazines, and I had them all lined up on the shelf, sorted by year. I decided to go through every one of them—seven years' worth—and write down every tip on power I found. It took me two weeks, and I ended up with 397 of them. Then I went through the list and crossed off all the duplications. I quickly realized that there really weren't that many new ideas in golf instruction. Everybody was saying the same things, and some of the ideas were contradictory. Did you switch to a stronger grip to keep from slicing it, or a weaker grip to release the club more aggressively? Was a wider stance better for more stability, or a narrow stance better because it helped you shift your weight? Should you cock your wrists early or late? I'd slam my hands down on the table when I was reading this stuff, because it was so frustrating to try to figure out which was the right tip.

Once I had a list of unique tips, I went to the range and spent hundreds of hours trying every one of them. If one worked, it made it onto my "keeper" list. If it didn't, I crossed it off and moved on to the next one. Once I condensed all the tips and boiled them down to the ones that worked for me, I was ready. I had my Bible.

I'd go practice, and if I was hitting it bad, I'd go to the book. When the pages of tips started to wear out, I typed them up onto small pieces of paper and had them laminated. I had the pages bound into a small black notebook that I carry with me in my golf bag to this day, so I can refer to it whenever I need to. I kept another notebook, and I recorded the date when I had certain problems and what the fixes were. I wrote down what clubhead and shaft combinations worked and which ones didn't. Every year, I put at the front of that notebook what my goals were for the year—everything from ball speed to the number of balls I wanted to average in play on the grid. I also kept track of every shot I hit in competition—where it ended up and how far it went. I could map where my shots were going and use my practice time to hit more of the shots that were going long and erase the mistakes. I discovered that all my longest shots were on the left side of the grid, so I practiced aiming right and hitting pulls on purpose, to get more yards.

By the time I started preparing for the National Championship in the fall of 1995, I had a list of core tips that always worked and a list of current tips that were clicking with me at the time. In 1995, I was working on slowing down my takeaway and not turning my hips on the backswing. By gaining such a clear sense of what I needed to do with my swing, I had more time to practice competition scenarios. I practiced different scenes in my mind and tried to make it as real as possible, so that when I got into the situation my mind would feel like it had been there before and would be better suited to relaxing and performing at a high level.

I was still scraping by, working as a district manager for a human resources company at this point, and the 1995 championship was going to be my last shot at trying to make this long-drive thing work. My wife, Karen, and I drove five hours from Little Rock to Huntsville, Alabama, for the local qualifier. Back then, you paid $30 for each set of six balls you hit to try to make it through. As long as you kept paying, you could keep hitting. Since only eight guys were competing, one guy was going to make it through. I was stuck hitting into a headwind, and the best I could do was 350 yards, two behind a guy who had caught one with a tailwind.

I was out of cash, and Karen and I had maxed out our credit cards just to make the trip, so it looked like I was going to go home and try to focus on my real job. But some kind people in the stands said they knew I was the longest hitter but just had bad luck with the wind, so they put up $30 each to bring the field to ten, which got the top two finishers in. Karen and I got back in the car to drive to Little Rock with no money and no credit, and then the clutch went out. We tried everything to get the car working again—I even whacked the engine with a softball bat I had in the trunk. Finally we got it rolling down the hill, started it in gear, and managed to limp home, but when Karen says we were living on love, she wasn't joking.

The district tournament was in Biloxi, Mississippi, and the edge of Hurricane Erin hit just in time to put me into a 40-mile-per-hour headwind. My longest drive there was 295 yards, which was second best, but only the number one qualifier made it through. I was crushed, and pretty much convinced that I shouldn't be spending any more money trying to chase this dream. Back in Little Rock, I had put my clubs away for good when the phone rang. It was the Long Drivers of America, saying they had decided to take two qualifiers from each district. I was in the championship. I had the shortest qualifying drive of any of the guys who made it to the main event, but still, I was in the championship.

A week before the event, I had a bad car accident. An elderly woman turned in front of me and smashed up my car. My left knee went through the dash and touched the battery, and my head smashed the windshield (having a hard head is a benefit sometimes, I guess). I also cracked my sternum and broke the middle finger on my right hand. So when I got to Las Vegas, I can promise you that nobody was thinking I was a threat to win the championship. I was staying in the Las Vegas Hilton, and the sports book there had me at 6-to-1 odds, lumped in with a group of other guys who were basically field bets. I put $20 down on myself—if you don't have confidence in yourself, who will?—and went to work.

My strategy for that tournament came directly out of the work I had been doing with my Long-Drive Bible. I practiced hitting six balls in two groups of three. On the first three, my goal was to hit a solid shot that got me on the board. In the second three, I was trying to smoke one. It worked perfectly, just like I practiced. I made my way through the qualifying rounds—even though I almost had to withdraw three times because I couldn't close my hand all the way with the broken finger—to get to the final group of six, broadcast on ESPN, for the first time in my career. Instead of getting more nervous with each round passing, I actually got less nervous. The way I figured, I had nothing to lose, and I was already surpassing anything I had done before.

In the finals, I hit my first ball 346 yards, which was good for second place, four behind the leader. Then, on the fourth ball—my first ball of the second set of three—I crushed it right down the middle 362 yards. That drive broke the twenty-three-year-old distance record of 353 yards, set by Evan "Big Cat" Williams, and my margin of victory over Bruce Evans, 12 yards, was also the biggest in the history of the championship.

After I won that first title, I knew I had what it took, and I set out to win it again. I started planning how to make my living in the sport. Karen and I discussed how that could happen, and we decided that I had to replace my and her income. It seemed like all the money in the world, but we both knew that we wanted her to be home full-time, to give our kids something we didn't have when we were growing up. Karen was pregnant with our first child, Beau, during the 1995 championship. Palmer came in 1999, and Paige was born in 2002.

I won my second world championship in 2001 in dramatic fashion and had my endorsements in place. I was finally in position to make some serious money.

This sport is wide, in terms of the number of guys who are trying to "make it." Every year, more than 14,000 guys start out in local qualifying to try to get to the RE/MAX World Championship in October. But the number of guys who can actually say they're long driving, and only long driving, to support themselves? There might only be four or five. I'm proud to say I'm one of them. I do between eighty and one hundred exhibitions a year, and I've got great sponsorship deals in place with Dunlop for my equipment and JLG for my shafts. I don't have the nicest house in Little Rock, but we've got the complete cable package at home and my wife drives a nice car. We can even order pizza pretty much whenever we want. Don't laugh: when Karen and I were first married, any kind of takeout food was a big luxury. I'm extremely proud of being a self-made guy, and I wouldn't change anything. I've eaten enough food from a can to last me for a while.

Coming up with the Bible was obviously the difference between being just another big guy trying to hit it far and a three-time world champion. But I really got more out of it that that. At the beginning of my career, I spent a lot of time searching for the right move or the right feel. It finally dawned on me that if I could sort out the answers, I didn't have to experiment as much. Just for longevity purposes it's been a huge bonus. I beat balls—thousands of them at a time—to the point where I needed multiple cortisone shots every year. There were times when I couldn't lift a glass of milk.

Physically, it's starting to get to me. I've torn the rotator cuffs in both shoulders—in fact, the one in my left shoulder is torn right now, as I type this. I've had sports hernias, groin tears, degenerating disks in my back. I have to get two sets of epidurals a year to keep hitting these days—but that's better than the year I had twenty-four cortisone shots. The knuckle at the base of my left thumb swells up every time I hit more than a few balls. My right wrist is so bad that I have to almost immobilize it with tape before I do an exhibition. I could get surgery, but that's a risk. It might not ever be right again.

Now the only serious ball-beating I do is in the month leading up to the World Championship. At that point, I'm trying to get myself into hitting shape, so I can have the endurance to hit the last ball on the fifth day of the event with as much energy, power, and concentration as I did the first one in the first qualifying round.

In that run-up to the tournament, I'm on the ninth tee at Chenal Country Club, my club in Little Rock, hitting drivers from 7 a.m. to 9:15, when the first group arrives. I use the ninth hole because it's 512 yards long, and it forces me to hit to a target—a target that's about the same width as the grid at the World Championship. When play gets to my tee, I go straight to the range and hit for another 90 minutes, then take a break. Then I hit all afternoon. On days when I don't hit, I'm in the weight room. The rest of the year, I'm trying to preserve my body. Hey, I'm in my mid-forties now. It sucks getting old. I don't know how much longer I can do it, but I'm going to find out. I've always said that I'm going to keep doing this until I hit my best ball and get beat. That hasn't happened yet.

Honestly, I go up and down the line now at the World Championship and I see dozens of guys who can do things physically that I could never do. They're bigger than I am—and younger. I'm 6 foot 5 and weigh 245. When I started out in the early 1990s I was one of the bigger guys. At the finals in 2005, I looked up at more than half of them. John Coburn is 6' 10". Kurt Moore is 6' 8". Viktor Johansson, who is from Sweden, is 6' 6" and weighs 280, and his arms are as big around as my head.

Some of those guys are starting to figure the sport out, but most of them? They're just beating balls. They don't have a plan. They're searching, just like I was. When I get out there, I'm pulling out three balls, thinking about my swing keys, then hitting them. Then I'm pulling out my second set of three balls and doing it again. I'm trying to hit balls in the grid. That's where the money is.

Thanks to the Bible, I can find the grid a lot quicker. And now you can, too.

The second question I always get, after "How far can you hit it?" is "Yeah, but what do you shoot?" Now, I'm thinking you didn't buy this book to hear me talk about how to hit your chip shots closer or smooth out your putting stroke. But since you asked, I can play a little bit. At Chenal, we've got two courses. On the wide-open one, my handicap is plus-two, and I shot an eight-under 64 there once. Don't get me wrong—I know how good those Tour guys are, and I know my place. Those guys are golfers. I'm a long driver. I'm accurate within the parameters of my sport, but guys like Tiger Woods and Phil Mickelson have a lot more control of the ball than I do. On the tighter course at Chenal, I'm a five handicap. They put some million-dollar homes in danger pretty close to the fairways over there, and the landing areas on some of those holes are only 20 or 30 yards deep—deep, not wide. It's one thing to worry about spraying it left or right. On that course, I have to find some place for the ball to land on the other side of a dogleg. When you're swinging all out, it's hard to judge the difference between, say, 330 and 350 yards.

I'll bet that's a problem you'd like to have.

3

THE TEN COMMANDMENTS OF DISTANCE

How did I go from 397 different *Golf Digest* tips down to my Ten Commandments of Distance? Time, sweat, blisters, and a ton of frustration. And getting to the set of tips and swing thoughts that made up my first Long-Drive Bible in 1995 was only the first step.

The commandments you see here are the result of all that work in 1995, but also the twelve years of competing and practicing that have come since then. I'm constantly working through the pages of my Bible, refining the tips that work and replacing others with ones that are better. I'm also always looking for the most stream-lined way to help people in the clinics and corporate outings. That constantly pushes me to take what I do with my own swing and translate it so that the average guy can understand it and use it.

The list I've come up with here—the Ten Commandments—is simple. It starts with your stance and ball position and proceeds in order, through your backswing, transition, downswing, and finish. There's a lot of detail in the rest of the book on things like slicing and equipment, but I truly believe you can take the information contained in these Ten Commandments and immediately get 20 yards longer. I've seen it happen for sixty-year-old guys who hit it 185 yards and twenty-five-year-old guys who hit it 260. Spend an afternoon at the range trying these tips out one by one, and by the end of the day you'll be shocked at how much more clubhead speed you can generate. It's in there. We just have to find it.

1. Take a wide stance.

It always amazes me to see how much effort the average guy puts into his swing. Unfortunately, most of that effort is wasted, because it's applied the wrong way and from a setup position that makes it almost impossible to consistently generate clubhead speed.

I don't think it's because the average player doesn't have an idea of how to set up to the ball. It's more a combination of incomplete—and just plain bad—advice. Let's start with stance width. I've seen plenty of instruction articles that say a narrow stance, with the feet hip-width apart, is good for power, because it encourages weight transfer on the backswing and the downswing. There were plenty of stance tips in the group of 397 I started with in 1995. I see the results of that bad advice all the time: a player with his feet close apart, tipping backward on the backswing, then sliding his hips toward the target on the downswing, or worse, hanging back and making a reverse pivot.

When I worked construction, I saw a lot of backhoes—you know, the yellow tractors with the big scoop arm coming out of the back. And when that backhoe needed stability to lift a heavy load, it had these metal legs that extended from the sides to brace it. I think a golf swing needs that kind of stability, especially if you're going to generate some speed.

You need to be anchored in the ground and pivot around a fixed point to be able take advantage of the chain reaction between your hips, chest, arms, and hands. From a wide base—with your feet a little bit wider than your shoulders—you get that stability. If your stance is too narrow, you're going to rock and tip. And from that narrow platform, it's easy for you to take the club back inside (pull the club toward you in relation to the target line), then loop it straight up and over the top and slap across the ball. If you're hitting a weak slice, you know exactly what I'm talking about. I think the only time you should use a narrow stance is on a short pitch shot, when you're concerned more with touch than with generating speed. You don't take the club back very far on that shot, and there's no real danger of losing your balance.

Another way to visualize what I'm talking about is to watch Ichiro hit a baseball and then watch Albert Pujols hit one. Ichiro starts out with a narrower stance, and he basically runs forward and slashes at the ball as it comes over the plate. He's got tremendous hand-eye coordination, and he's trying to make contact, put the ball in play, and use his speed. Pujols has a much wider, more anchored stance, and he makes a strong pivot around his braced front leg and just hammers the ball with a compact, ultra-fast swing. If you want to hit your tee shots longer, you want to be like Pujols. If you want to hit your tee shots like Ichiro, you probably need to buy another book.

The other thing the average player hears a lot is that he needs to set up with the right shoulder lower than the left, so he can hit the ball on the upswing. That's solid advice, but it's incomplete. If you think of your shoulders and spine as a T shape, you need to tilt that entire letter T, so that your spine is angled away from the target. That puts your right shoulder lower than your left. Most players

My right shoulder is lower than my left by about three inches, and my spine is tilted away from the target. Be careful not to just shift your shoulder down without tilting your spine. That's a common mistake.

I like a wide platform to hit from, so I can feel stable through my swing. If you were going try to move something heavy, like a refrigerator, you'd do it with your feet apart, not set narrow.

hear that they need to tilt, and they leave the spine at a 90-degree angle to the ground and just cock the shoulders. When you do that, it restricts your arm swing away from the ball and keeps your arms trapped close to your body.

Go through the following process every time you set up and you won't have a problem. First, set your feet wider than shoulder-width apart, as if you were a shortstop waiting to field a ground

Most average players set up with their feet too close together, like this. This stance would work for a wedge shot, but you need to support a bigger turn and a more violent downswing with your driver.

ball. Drop your right shoulder three inches. Bring your left shoulder forward so that it's in line with your right shoulder and parallel to the line between your ball and your target (hold your club across your chest at shoulder height to check this line). Then tuck your right elbow in until it's about two inches from your right hip. Make sure your right elbow is bent and relaxed, while your left arm is more rigid. It should feel like you're reaching out to hold a doorknob with your left hand and you're ready to throw a ball sidearm under that left arm with your right hand.

How you set your feet also makes a big impact on how fast you can swing it. I make sure to keep my right foot square to the target line, for two reasons. I want to limit my hip turn on the backswing and create torque with a big shoulder turn (the so-called X factor, or the difference in degrees between how far you rotate your hips and your shoulders). More X factor means more power. It's as simple as that. A square right-foot position also helps me push off on the downswing in the same way a pitcher uses the mound for leverage. If you flare the right foot out, away from the target, you lose that leverage point, and that's a power leak.

You want the lead foot to do the opposite of what you want from the back foot, which means you want to flare it out toward the target three or four inches, so you can fire your hips through faster. Don't overdo it, though, or you'll hit a big push to the right.

With good shoulder tilt, square alignment, and foot position, you have a much better chance of swinging on a flatter, more sweeping plane into the ball. You also put less sidespin on the ball that way, and it's much easier to keep your balance at every point in the swing. Then all you have to do is put the ball in the right place to get in the way of the clubhead when it's going the fastest.

2. Tee it up forward and high.

The first thing you'll find when you set up in the position I'm showing you in the good setup photograph in Commandment No. 1 (see the figure on the right on page 40) is that putting your driver down on the ground in front of you will direct you to the right place to tee up your ball. It'll probably be way more forward than you're used to—off your left big toe. That's because you want to sweep through and hit the ball on the upswing (which we're going to talk about in one of the other commandments). Most players play the ball far too close to the middle of the stance with the driver.

Most players generate their peak clubhead speed right as the shaft passes the middle of the front leg. Knowing that, why would you want to set up with the ball behind that? Not only are you wasting speed, but the club hasn't fully squared up on its way around your body, either. You'll hit it lower and more to the right unless you compensate by flipping your hands at it.

You also need to move the ball forward in your stance when you use a driver because you're hitting the shot off a tee. With an iron, you want the club to bottom out just beyond the ball. You're hitting that shot with a descending blow. With a driver, you want to hit the ball *after* the club has bottomed out, when it's on the slight upswing. With the ball teed up in the air, the club is coming from below the ball up into it, which is how you launch it higher than the loft number that's written on your club.

Ball position for a driver is a natural extension of where you have it for other clubs. With your short irons, you play the ball in the middle of your stance, because a short-iron swing is a steep up-and-down swing. As the club gets longer, your stance gets wider and your shoulders tilt more away from the target, so the swing gets more sweeping and less up-and-down. For a long iron or a hybrid, ball position should be a couple of inches inside your left toe. So it makes sense that when you get to your driver, with the ball teed up in the air, you want to be up at your big toe.

One thing to keep in mind is that you need to have good shoulder tilt to be able to reach that forward ball position at address. If you don't tilt, you'll have to stretch your right arm to reach the ball, and that pulls your right shoulder closer to the target line. When your shoulders open that way, you're going to hit a slice.

You've probably heard that you need to tee the ball higher now because of how tall the big 460 cc driver heads are these days. That's definitely true, but the common advice you hear—tee it so that half the ball is showing above the top of the clubhead—isn't sufficient.

Letting your ball position with the driver drift back toward the center is a common mistake. From here, the club doesn't have a chance to get square on the downswing, and you'll tend to hit the ball low and right.

With the ball forward in your stance, off your left big toe, the shaft of the club will feel like an extension of your left arm.

The USGA limits tee height to four inches. I use four-inch Zero Friction tees, and I barely stick them in the ground. The result is that the ball is completely above the face of my driver at address. The way I look at it, it's like hitting a ball off a building. If you're higher up, the ball is going to travel farther than if you're at ground level, because the launch point is higher off the ground. Now, with a four-inch tee, you're not talking about a huge advantage, but in a long drive, every inch counts.

Even with a full-size 460 cc driver, teeing the ball up so half of it is above the clubhead isn't taking enough advantage.

The USGA limits tees to four inches long. I stick my tee barely in the ground to get the ball teed up as high as I can. That way you can hit it with a powerful upward swing.

46   THE LONG-DRIVE BIBLE

More important, having the ball teed up that high definitely helps reinforce the idea that you need to hit it on the upswing. If you tee it up that high and don't swing that way, you're going to gouge a big scrape in the top of your club. By making sure you set your stance wide at address and tilt your spine, you're already in good shape to make that ascending blow on the ball. The tee helps you take advantage of that.

3. Keep your wrists "oily."

One of the best power tips I ever got came while I was watching a baseball game on television. Nolan Ryan was throwing a shutout, and every time they cut to a shot of him on the mound getting ready to pitch, he was shaking his pitching hand next to his side, as if he was trying to get some water off it.

After I watched for a while, I figured out what he was doing. He was trying to keep his arm and hand loose, because that's where the speed came from. Loose muscles move faster. When they asked Sam Snead the secret to his swing, he said a similar thing, that he wanted to feel "oily."

The key to hitting it hard is to be as tension-free as you can. Anytime you can see the veins or muscles in your arms, you know you're hanging on to it way too tight. You want your grip pressure to be about a two on a scale of one to ten. That's hard to do sometimes, especially under pressure. I know my grip tended to get tight at the beginning of my career.

When I watch the average guy hit a shot, he might have good mechanics and a pretty good move through the ball, but he's hanging on to the club so tightly that he doesn't have a chance to get any snap through impact. He's basically squeezing the life out of his hands and robbing himself of some clubhead speed that's right there for the taking. He's keeping centrifugal force from helping him.

There are a few situations where you might want to hold on to it tighter, like on a short pitch shot. But if power is the goal, you need to be loose and you need to use your hands. Then the club can release naturally—and fast—through impact.

The way you set your grip can have a big impact on how naturally you can let the club snap through impact. By far, the most

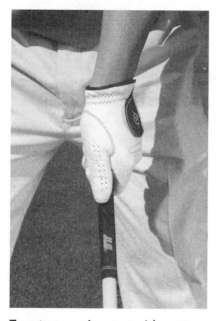

To set your grip, start with your left hand. You want your thumb to sit slightly on the right side of the top of the grip.

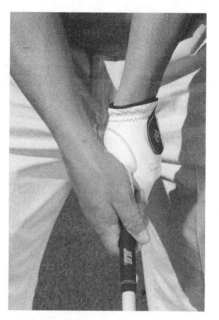

The right hand goes on in a slightly stronger position than the left, so that the V between the thumb and the side of the hand points just right of your right collarbone.

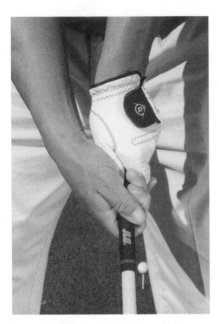 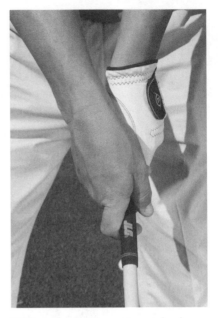

In a too-strong grip, your right hand is almost under the handle, and the V is pointed to the outside edge of your right shoulder. It's hard to get the club to release from this position.

With a weak grip, you can look down and see the top of your left hand. The club will tend to come through impact open with this grip.

common grip for the average player is one where the hands are turned to the right, in a strong position. When you look down at your hands on the grip, if the Vs created by your thumbs and the sides of your palms are pointed toward your right shoulder, you've got a strong grip.

Now, most players with an extremely strong grip have been told that they need to turn their hands that way to beat a slice. And it's true that a *slightly* strong grip will help you get the club square through impact. But if you shift your hands too far to the right, you take away all the wrist action in your swing. That actually makes it *harder* to square the clubface at impact, and it takes away a lot of the hand speed and snap that translates into big tee shots.

I like a grip that's neutral to slightly strong in the left hand and slightly more strong in the right hand. Start by placing your left hand on the grip so that the thumb sits just slightly to the right side of the top of the grip. The V we talked about should be pointed toward your right collarbone. Next, put your right hand on the grip so that the V points just outside your right collarbone. You'll feel the top of your right wrist in a flat position. It won't be bowed outward or cupped.

If you let your right hand go on too strong, that means it's over too much to the side of the handle. You'll feel the top of your wrist bow outward. If you put your hand on in too weak of a position, where the V is pointed at your chin, you'll be able to see much more of the top of your left hand. You want to be able to look down and see two knuckles.

When it comes to using an interlocking grip versus an overlapping grip, I'm in favor of whatever makes you comfortable and whatever keeps your hands solidly on the club. I use an overlapping grip—where the little finger on my right hand rests on top of my left hand, between my index and middle fingers, because it's closer to the grip I use to hit a softball. Tiger Woods uses an interlocking grip—where the little finger on the right hand interlocks with the index finger of the left hand—and so did Jack Nicklaus, so it's certainly possible to hit it hard that way, too. The most important thing is that your hands work together and don't slide around independent of each other on the grip.

4. Take it back low and slow.

What happens when you hit the ball is pretty much dictated by the first two feet of your swing. If you can get that part right, the downswing basically takes care of itself. Get off track and you have to do some serious rerouting to hit the ball solid. Two of the biggest mistakes I see amateur players make happen during this two-foot stretch.

The "death move" in a golf swing is picking the club straight up right away on the backswing. Do that and there's absolutely nothing good that can happen in your swing. Your arms will collapse close to your body (which we'll talk about next), and the club will have to come back down to the ball on a really steep angle and from outside the target line. You have no extension, no turn, and no speed at all.

The other problem during that first two feet of swing is tempo. If you get too aggressive with your hands at this early point in the swing, your tendency is to pull the club back around your body, flat and behind you. From there you have to throw your hands out toward the target line to get the club "unstuck" from behind you, and, again, you're going to come at the ball from a steep angle and from outside the target line.

Clubhead speed doesn't count until the foot or so behind the ball on the downswing, so don't go trying to generate it on your first move back. Practice a slow takeaway that feels like your hands are staying low to the ground. When the shaft is parallel to the ground on the backswing, the butt of the club should be pointing directly at where you're aiming. If you lift the club, the butt would be pointing straight down at this point. If you snatch the club back too fast, the butt would be pointing way to the right. What you're trying to do is take it back with your arms until your upper body

This is what extension looks like. My left arm is straight, and my right elbow is starting to bend a little bit. If you try to stretch your right arm out as well, you'll be in an awkward position that's difficult to turn from. When the club is parallel to the ground on the backswing, the butt end should point at the target.

starts to turn. The rest of your backswing will take care of itself at that point. One good thing to remember is that trying to "make" your arms move fast by jerking them around will only make the club move slower. You need to let your arms wind up and unwind because of what's happening with the rest of your body.

5. Keep your hands away from your chest.

I've got a hundred tricks to get more distance, but the one that is positively guaranteed to work for any player, no matter what he's built like, is this one. If you turn your shoulders more on your backswing and concentrate on keeping the butt end of the club as far away from the middle of your sternum as possible, you'll pick up 20 yards on your tee shot. You'll have to practice it a little bit, because it definitely takes some effort to push your left arm out there, but those yards are guaranteed.

If you try to keep both arms straight in the backswing instead of stretching your left arm and letting the right one fold, both arms will collapse back close to your body when you get to the top of your backswing. This is not a powerful position.

Keep turning and push the club away from your chest with your left arm while letting the right arm fold. That's the key to good extension.

The key is to stay wide with your left arm and let your right arm bend as you turn. Most players get into trouble when they try to keep both arms straight on the backswing, in a misguided attempt to get "extension." When you do that, you get into a very awkward position when it comes time to turn your shoulders, and both of your arms collapse close to your body. To simplify the physics, the wider your radius (the length of your left arm), the more time you have to generate clubhead speed on your downswing, and the more leverage you have to generate that speed. If you let the radius get short (when the left arm collapses and bends), you have less time and less leverage. Remember, you're looking for left arm extension. That's the key to clubhead speed. One feel I like is that

When the arms collapse, it's basically a given that the club will come back to the ball steeply and from outside the target line.

I'm pushing the butt end of the club away from my chest with my left arm as I make my shoulder turn on the backswing.

6. Turn your left shoulder over your right knee at the top.

A reverse pivot is the curse of a ton of average golfers. It happens mostly because you're tilting your shoulders the opposite way you're supposed to—with the left moving down toward the ball on the backswing and the right shoulder lifting. That sends your weight forward, toward the target, on your backswing—the opposite direction it should be going—and then back, away from the target, during the downswing. You can't physically hit a ball more than 200 yards that way.

This is what a reverse pivot looks like. It starts with the club lifting straight up . . .

. . . and the left shoulder dipping, so the weight shifts forward on the backswing.

At the top, there's no shoulder turn, and the arms have collapsed close to the body.

On a good backswing, the weight is on the right instep, and my shoulder has turned over my right knee.

The simple key to fixing it is thinking about your left shoulder position as you make your backswing. I want you to turn your left shoulder so that it's over your right knee at the top of the backswing. If you do that, so many good things will happen in your swing. You won't slide. Your head will be in great position—behind the ball—to really make a strong move through impact. And you'll be developing tremendous coil and leverage.

I know what you're thinking: "I'm not flexible enough to do that." That's just not true. I'm not at all flexible, and I can do it. For some people, it's easier to think about turning the right shoulder back, but either way, it's a move you'll be able to make with about 20 minutes' practice on the range.

7. Rotate, don't slide.

We've already talked about how the club should snap at the bottom of the downswing, as though you cracked a whip. Now, if you moved the whole handle of the whip back and forth as fast as you could, you'd never generate any speed at the whip end. The concept is the same when you turn back and through in your swing. If you slide your hips back, away from the target, then slide them through, you don't have a stable base to crack the whip at impact. You're wasting your turning speed and making it hard to hit the ball consistently square, too. In all the sports I've played, the best results come when you keep the center of rotation stable through the swing. That doesn't change if you're trying to hit a softball, throw a javelin, or hit a golf ball. When you slide, the rotation isn't

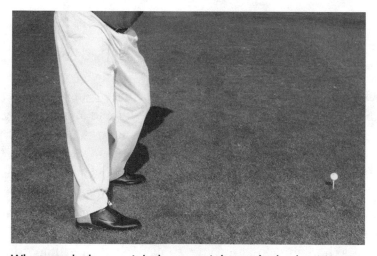

When you lock your right knee straight on the backswing, it's far easier to slide on your backswing instead of turn.

With your right knee bent, you can't slide too far back, away from the target, on your downswing because there's no way to support your weight. It's a great trick to use to stop yourself from sliding instead of turning.

happening at a stable point, and you can't use the natural effects of centrifugal force to help you.

Okay, that was a mouthful. What does that mean in real life? It's simple. Try flexing your back knee a little bit and angling it slightly toward your left knee at address. When you do that, you won't be able to slide on the backswing. There's no way to support that sliding move. It's incredible how much more stable you'll feel over the ball. You'll make your turn above the ball instead of sliding back and through. When you try this, it'll be like somebody turned a power switch on in your golf swing.

The other unfortunate thing a tall, locked right knee does is push your right shoulder higher in your backswing. We've already talked about why that's bad—it makes it hard for you to make a sweeping upswing through the ball.

8. Tighten your downswing angle. (This is called "snap.")

The golf instruction library is filled with books and articles about "lag," the angle between your arms and the shaft as you swing down from the top. I've read a bunch of them that say you should somehow hold on to that angle as long as you can, and that's the key to distance. That's partially true, but again, I don't think it's the whole story.

I don't believe your conscious thought should be "holding" your wrist cock through your downswing. If anything, that's going to slow down the natural release of your wrists—the "snap" that creates so much extra power. What I want you to do is actually set your wrists at the top and fully cock them, then make the right first move on the way down. If you do that, the centrifugal force of your body turning is first going to create more lag in your backswing automatically, then pull the club straight as you swing through impact. In other words, you should be working with physics, not against it.

I'm actually going to use a bad word when it comes to golf instruction—casting. When a teacher tells you you're casting, he means you're releasing the club at the wrong time. You're releasing the angle between the shaft and your left arm at the top of your swing. But you actually *want* to cast the club in your swing. It's just that you want to do it when you're down by the ball.

The one thing I've always been able to relate to is the idea of casting a lure from a john boat. If you've ever been on one, you know a john boat is pretty unstable, and you also know you'll get a dirty look from your buddy if you use a bunch of body movements

If I don't cock my wrists at the top, there are no creases at the base of my right thumb, and my left thumb is pointed straight up in the air. I'm costing myself a lot of power and wrist snap at impact.

to throw that lure out there, because a wobbly boat scares away the fish. To cast the lure from that boat, you've got to flick your wrists. That wrist flick is exactly the snap I use at the bottom of my swing. Notice I said *bottom*. If you release that angle too early, that's when you get the flip move that so many players struggle with—the one that adds loft to your shots and makes you hit a weak fade.

One swing thought that has really worked with the amateur players I play with is thinking about the hole in the bottom of the grip and what to do with it. I tell them to take that hole and think about driving it right down into the ball on the downswing. That doesn't make you hold your wrist cock or anything like that, but it makes you turn your body first to keep the club more behind you,

In a good wrist cock at the top, my wrists cock up,
so that my left thumb points at my head. My wrists *do not*
bend back and forth (cupping and bowing), like you'd slap
somebody—a common mistake. Try to create big creases at
the base of your right thumb at the top of your backswing.
Then you'll know you made a good wrist cock.

so you can drive the butt end downward, instead of yanking it out in front of you.

I've seen high-speed video (where the camera shoots at high speed so the image can be slowed down) of my hands through impact, and it's fascinating what they do. When my hands get close to impact, my arms actually seem to slow down almost to a stop, while my hands uncock and roll into basically an explosion. The better I set my wrists at the top, the more speed I can generate with my snap at the bottom.

One important thing to remember about wrist cock is that it should happen up and down, like flicking a fishing rod, and not back and forth, like you'd wave your hand to get a fly away from your food. You want the creases at the base of your right thumb and the *side* of your wrist to appear and disappear, not the ones on the underside of your wrist.

9. Keep your head behind the ball at impact.

An old long-driving buddy of mine, Mike Dunaway, gave me this swing thought, and it's worked very well over the years. He asked me if I ever saw an old lady beating a rug hanging over a clothesline. I scratched my head and said yes, I had. He told me to imagine that I was standing in my address position with that rug hanging down right in front of my left shoulder. The goal is to swing without

Here my body is shifting toward the target before my downswing has even gotten a quarter of the way completed. I'm only going to be able to hit the ball with arm speed.

With my head behind, I can sling the clubhead through with both arm and hand speed. It's just like a catapult multiplying the swinging force and throwing a rock a lot farther than a man could with his arm alone.

bumping your shoulder into the rug. That means you're keeping your head behind the ball at impact. The first thing that should hit that rug is the clubhead. If your shoulders hit it or your hands hit it, that means you're moving in front of the ball and pushing it. You'll never get a good release and the full catapult effect of the club unwinding through the ball that way.

Another image I use a lot is that I'm standing in my address position with my head inside a broken window not much bigger than my head. There's jagged glass all around the frame of the window, and if I dip my head or move it back on my backswing, I'm going to cut myself up pretty good. Essentially, what I'm trying to do is keep my head still and my left ear behind the ball until after I hit it. With your head back, you're letting the arms and the club unwind against a brace—like that whip cracking—and build the most speed possible. Move your head forward and you lose the benefit of that pivot and brace. Then the ball will move only as fast as you can muscle it. Think about how much easier it is to move a boulder with a lever and a pivot point than by just bending over and trying to shove it out of the way with your back muscles.

10. Stay in balance.

I hope I've been able to reinforce the point that shoving the club around in your backswing and downswing doesn't do anything to help you generate speed. I want you to hit the ball harder, but without overswinging or lunging it at it with a big upper-body move early in the downswing.

I call that lunge the "Beast Factor," and I see it all the time in pro-ams—and even at the World Championship. It usually happens right after a guy tells me (proudly) how far he can hit it, and he wants to show off for the long-drive guy. I can see him grip up on it—squeezing the grip tighter—and then make a big lateral sway off the ball. He lurches his weight back past the outside of his right foot, then throws the clubhead hard from the top and casts it with a big lunge toward the ball with his upper body. The over-the-top move adds loft and puts a big slice on it, so he either goes ahead and hits a big banana ball, or he feels it coming and flips his hands over and hits a big snap hook. That's almost always followed by an "I never hit it like that" comment, or a retee before the first ball even hits the ground.

At the World Championship level, when a guy gets really charged up and out of control, his backswing gets really fast. Because the guys in this sport are so strong, that speed going back wobbles the shaft when the club changes direction at the top of the backswing. Believe it or not, the wobble is enough to send the club off-plane on the way down—even with the super-stiff shafts we use. My shafts have extra boron right under the grip, because I used to actually snap them because I made such a fast transition.

When the shaft kicks too early, the only way to try to save the shot is to manipulate the hands and guess. Since he can't release naturally, with his regular timing, that shot just isn't going to be as long—which is ironic, because the whole point of cranking it back like that is to really bomb one. There should be no more effort on the backswing than it would take to pick a salt shaker up off the table and put it on the shelf. Don't stress the shaft up at the top. You want that snap to be at the bottom.

When I make a full finish, my weight is centered over my left foot and my hips are turned past square to the target, so that they're actually pointing left of where I'm aiming. The centrifugal force of my swing pulls me up into this position.

It doesn't matter how many times I say it, but it's still true. Controlled, balanced aggression is what generates a big tee shot. The best way to test yourself to see if you're staying in balance is to check yourself at finish. If you can use your clubhead speed to pull yourself up into a balanced finish position that you can hold without falling over, you're sequencing your swing the right way.

The Ten Commandments cover all the basics you need to hit the ball longer than you ever did before. I've seen it happen over the space of five or six balls on the driving range with guys I'm spending the day with at an outing.

You're probably thinking to yourself, "These commandments are nice, but where do the 350-yard tee shots come from? How can some guys hit it so far? How can *I* hit it that far?" Sorry to say, but this is where the cruel part of sports comes in.

I believe every player has a maximum speed he can swing the club—which means he's got a "number" that's pretty much the biggest tee ball he's going to be able to hit, where he says, "That's all I've got." I win world championships because I get right up close to my max number, and my max number is very high—about 375 yards of carry under normal conditions. There are less than ten guys in the world who can say that. That's because of the hand speed and "snap" I get at impact. How fast you can uncock your wrists at impact is the last piece of the swing-acceleration puzzle. Turning big and uncoiling efficiently will get you plenty of power, but the amount of snap you can generate separates the men from the boys, so to speak. You're pretty much stuck with the maximum speed potential you're born with. My goal with this book is to get you swinging as close as possible to that maximum speed.

In 1997 I took a trip to Motion Reality Sports in Marietta, Georgia, to go through a session on the swing analysis machine they have down there. They covered me with motion sensors and had me hit balls in an indoor hitting bay surrounded by nets. Before I got started, the technicians asked me what I thought were the specific reasons I could hit the ball so far. I told them I didn't know; I had just always been long. They told me they had twenty-five years of swings from the PGA Tour on their computers, and the sensors were going to be able to point out exactly where my power came from.

Well, once I got warmed up, some eyes got really big in the laboratory. I hit my third ball completely through the netting, and it went bouncing around the studio, just missing thousands of dollars' worth of equipment. They brought in a second net, but we still had to stop three different times so they could recalibrate the machines to be able to capture my body and clubhead movement.

Every once in a while, I'd hear an "Oh my God" or "Holy shit" from over by the monitor after I really killed one. I'm used to getting comments like that when someone first sees what I can do to a golf ball, but these guys were experts, and I thought they would have seen some other fast swings.

After they got the machine dialed in, I think they were just mesmerized by what was happening. They kept asking me if I could go any faster. Well, at this point in my career I was hitting a thousand balls a day and loving every minute of it, so I dialed it up as fast as I could go—until I tore the skin on three fingers and broke the blood vessels around my eyes three hours later.

At the end, they printed out my results. My top clubhead speed was 171.2 miles per hour, from a sensor they put on the toe of the clubhead. I've still got the printout. That was the fastest they had ever measured, but what really blew the technicians away was how the graphs for the sensors on my hands were distorted. That was because I snapped the club so fast through impact that the machine couldn't recognize the movement. I had the fastest hand speed they had ever recorded, by far.

Being 6 foot 5 and 245 pounds is nice, but fast hands are the reason I can do this for a living. You'll just have to be satisfied with the 20 extra yards I find you for your driver. That's not so bad, is it?

4

FIX YOUR SLICE

We've gone through my Ten Commandments for hitting the ball longer, and if you followed them, you're definitely stepping off more yardage from the tee. But what if you're still losing shots to the right, even if your contact is a lot more solid than it was before? What if you're a slicer? I know, it's a dirty word, but slicing is far and away the most common ball flight for the average player. And you know what? If you're a slicer, I really feel your pain.

Believe it or not, I've always been a slicer. When I've hit my biggest drives in competition, it's because I've adjusted enough to be able to aim for the right side of the grid and hit a pull down the left side (and when I miss it, it's usually over in the right trees, by the generators and the construction equipment). Any teacher will tell you that a pull is basically the same swing as a slice swing, but with the face closed instead of open.

When you and I hit that big slice, it's because we aren't getting the clubface square in time for impact. Even when your swing path is pretty good, if you're leaving that clubface open through impact—maybe the club isn't releasing because you've got a too-strong grip, or it isn't releasing enough because your grip is really weak—the ball will go right.

Because a slice can tend to creep in even more when you're swinging hard at it, I've got a whole page in my little black book filled with slice cures and swing thoughts. The World Championship lasts five days, and you have to make it through ten rounds to hold up that trophy. There've been plenty of times over the twenty years I've been in the championship that I've had to make some adjustments in between rounds because I knew I wasn't hitting it good enough to win. Most of the time, it's been because I was missing too many shots right. The slice cures in my little black book have saved me time and again, including at the 2005 championship, when I made it through the seventh round by only one yard.

Before the quarterfinals, I worked on pivoting around my right foot, and I went on to win my next heat. I was the second longest hitter in the semifinals, and I hit the longest ball in the finals, which is pretty good proof that these tips work. In this chapter, I'll tell you about my favorites (including the right foot pivot tip) and how you can use them to immediately stop losing it right. A lot of teachers want you to make changes to your swing path to fix a slice. Long-term, that's the best fix, but how does that help you when you're standing on the third tee and you've already made a couple double bogeys—or you're in the middle of a six-ball set at the World Championship?

You can break down these cures into two groups—swing thoughts and mechanical adjustments. When it comes to the swing thoughts, what we're really talking about are "feels," ideas that will help you get a better shape or rhythm to your swing. It doesn't matter how many times you hear that you need to stop coming over the top. When you're out there actually playing golf, that kind of advice doesn't really help you. Your swing is a chain reaction of movements. When you do one thing right (or wrong), it causes the next thing in the sequence to happen. So the right swing thought at the beginning, when you're getting ready to make your first move, can change the sequence.

1. Back off your effort to 85 percent.

One of the biggest power losses—and causes of a slice—comes when you try to "create" speed the wrong way. Whipping the club-head from the top of the backswing spends all of your speed too early, basically keeping you from cracking the whip at impact. When you hear a teacher tell you you're casting the club, that's what he means—your first move on the downswing is to fire your hands and uncock your wrists, instead of turning your hips and letting your upper body, arms, and club follow. The problem for most players, myself included, is that this casting move feels powerful. When you think to yourself, "I've got to pound one," it's tough to also think to yourself, "Wait for the lower body to go first."

I've talked to a lot of PGA Tour players, and almost to a man they say that when they need to hit a good, straight tee shot, they're thinking about swinging at most 85 percent power. They actually end up hitting it longer than if they "tried" to swing it faster, because the sequencing of motion is under so much more control and the muscles are more relaxed. Your balance is better, too, and you're going to hit more shots in the middle of the clubface. I'm not telling you that you should never swing hard. I'm a believer in using as much effort as you can while staying in balance. But if you're slicing it, the goal is to get your lower body turning ahead of your arms and hands in the downswing. Backing off your max effort makes that easier.

I use this tip as an important part of my strategy at the World Championship. Each round, we get six balls to hit in the grid, and if you don't get any in, you aren't going to advance. I break my six into two sets of three, and on the first sets I concentrate on making an 85 percent swing to get one on the grid in good shape. That frees me up to go after the second sets as hard as I can.

2. Square yourself to your target.

The way you hold the club has a huge impact on how you set up and, in turn, where your shots go. Because you hold the club with your right hand below your left, the tendency is to open your shoulders to make it easier for your lower arm to reach the lower point of the grip. It just feels better to set up this way. But open shoulders will tend to make you hit across the ball and curve it to the right. Set up to your tee shot, then hold your driver across your chest at mid-shoulder height. You'll probably see the club pointing left of where you thought you were aiming. To fix this open shoulder problem, simply tilt your spine away from the target a little more—in other words, lower your right shoulder. This will help your right arm get in a more comfortable position without your shoulders having to open up.

The evil thing about hitting a slice is that it will make you change your setup in subtle ways—without you even noticing. After you've seen a bunch of shots go flying 30 yards right of where you wanted them to go, it's only natural to start turning your shoulders more to the left to try to get the ball started out more that way. The problem is that when you turn your shoulders that way without adjusting your feet, you just make it worse. You cut across the ball even more, and even if it starts out a little more to the left, it's got so much sidespin on it that it actually curves more to the right than before. It's a vicious circle. You just start aiming your shoulders more left, and so on.

When your shoulders are open (the club on your chest would be pointing left of your target), the club wants to come back steep and straight up in your backswing. Your arms collapse close to your body, and you push your right shoulder out toward the target line

If you're a slicer, your tendency is to set up with your shoulders open, in an effort to get the ball started more to the left. The problem is, this just accentuates the move you're going to see in the next photograph.

The line of your shoulders is the line you swing along. So If your shoulders are open, you can't help but swing across the ball like this, which will cause you to either hit a big slice or a smother hook.

Adjust your setup position so that your shoulders are square to the target line. One way to check this is to set up, then hold your club across your chest at the shoulders. The club should point on a line parallel to the line you're aiming on.

and swing the club down steeply and across the target line. With those shoulders square, the club will move back lower and around you, and you'll be able to swing through on the inside path more easily.

When you go out to practice, lay one club down on the ground in front of your feet (on what's called your toe line) and put another one on the other side of the ball, parallel to both the target line and the club on your toe line. Then use a third club to hold across your chest after every five or six balls to make sure your shoulders aren't drifting open. That's a great habit to get into every time you practice. Go watch a PGA Tour event, and on the practice range you'll see several of the guys using guides like this when they're working on something after the round. I like it because it keeps you from drifting too open after two or three rounds out on the course. You'll also know that anything you're working on in your full swing will be from a solid, neutral setup position.

Once you start taking more care in where you set up in the tee box and how you actually aim yourself, you'll be amazed at how much more freely you can swing at the ball. I'm convinced that a lot of the indecision and steering of the ball that comes with a bad driving game is from a lack of confidence in where you're aiming, not because of any specific swing flaw.

3. Try a flatter swing.

Hitting a good tee shot is the same as hitting a home run in softball. In the softball swing, you're swinging flatter and around your body, with the bat coming through on the same plane as the ball is coming in. In golf, you can start to lose the ball right when your driver swing gets too up and down, because your right shoulder gets high on the backswing, and you tilt your shoulders up and down instead of turning them. Get the feel of a flatter turn and swing, and your arms will extend through the downswing much more easily. With that extra speed, the club will unwind naturally, instead of staying trapped under and cutting across the ball.

4. Make a straighter takeaway

Which part of the chain reaction causes the over-the-top move and a slice? Pulling the clubhead inside and behind you on the takeaway. Instead of concentrating on what you're supposed to be doing with the club during your transition—when it's going on too fast for you to do anything about it anyway—think about getting

On your takeaway, you want to make sure the club stays in line with the target for as long as possible and doesn't whip inside and behind you.

the butt of your club to point at the target for as long as possible on the takeaway. That will keep the clubhead from whipping back inside—the position where your only recovery is to throw it back out and over the top.

5. Lighten your grip.

Restricted hand action is the enemy of a straight ball. When you grip it tightly, you're actually preventing your hands from responding to centrifugal force and releasing the clubhead through impact. By your holding on, the club doesn't square up, and the ball will curve to the right. Feel like you're almost going to drop the club at address, and make a conscious effort to keep that light feel through your swing. I like to imagine that my glove is made out of paper and I'm trying to make my swing without ripping the paper. With that light grip, you'll get more hand action, wrist cock, and snap, which will get the clubface turning around square and your ball flying straight or with a draw.

6. Drop your right foot back and straighten the foot.

A slice comes from cutting across the ball from outside to in. One way to keep that from happening is to set yourself up so your path moves the other way, from inside to out. Drop your back foot back slightly from the target line (not dramatically—only about three inches) and make sure your foot is pointing straight out in front of you, not flared away from the target. This causes your hips and shoulders to close relative to your target line. Your swing path will tend to follow this closed line, so the club will come from the inside relative to where you want the ball to go. It's important not to overdo this by pulling your right foot back too far or by pulling your foot back but leaving your shoulders turned more open. If you pull your foot back too far, it's really easy to get too steep, and open shoulders will send the ball even more to the right.

7. Hood the face.

Probably the simplest fix on this list is to take your normal stance, then close the face of your driver a few degrees and retake your grip. This works well if you absolutely can't afford to miss on the right side. The disadvantage is that your trajectory is going to be lower because closing the face has the effect of taking loft off the

When I set up for a standard shot, the clubhead is square to the target.

If you're struggling with a slice, you can experiment with turning the toe in slightly at address. Put the club down behind the ball and turn it so the face is pointing more to the left. Then take your grip. Don't just turn the club to the left as you hold it in your grip. That will screw up your swing path.

club. One thing to keep in mind is that you want to set up to the ball with the face square, then actually turn the grip in your hands so that the face closes. If you hood the face by turning your hands instead, you're going to change your swing path. That will make you take the club back outside and cut across it, and you'll hit it even *more* to the right that way.

8. Shift more weight to the right (back) at address.

If you start out with your weight shifted left, toward the target, your tendency will be to lift the club straight up on the takeaway and reverse pivot on the downswing. Your weight will be moving back through impact—the opposite of what you want, and a big cause of a slice. By shifting more weight back at address, you can make a big turn and coil on the backswing and a conscious weight shift forward on the downswing. When your head stays back, behind the ball, through impact, you extend to the ball at impact and the club releases, and your slice disappears.

9. Swing around the right heel.

This tip is related to the previous one, in that it emphasizes staying behind the ball through impact. I always get strange looks when I give that piece of advice—staying behind it—because it sounds kind of like what happens when you reverse pivot. But there's a major difference. On a reverse pivot, your weight is actually moving *back*, away from the target. I want you to stay behind the ball, using your right heel as the centerpoint of your swing, and let the centrifugal force you create with the swing pull you through and stand you up into a perfect, balanced finish. That momentum you generate is more important than raw clubhead speed. I'll take a guy who can swing the club 135 miles per hour and maintain his momentum up through finish over a guy who can swing it 145 but is losing momentum because he's hanging back.

I used to have a lot more body action in my swing, and I wasn't getting as much out of it as I could. I have to give credit to Gerry James, one of my fellow competitors, for giving me this tip in 1994. He and I get along great (most of the time, and he can act like a four-year-old sometimes) because we're both willing to bust each other's chops, and we both tell it like it is.

10. Flatten the left wrist at the top of the backswing.

Of all the antislice keys I use, this one is the trickiest to get right away. Try it out on the driving range a few times before you bring it into play, because some players have a hard time visualizing exactly where their wrist is at the top. Basically, the position of your left wrist at the top determines whether your clubface is square, closed, or open at that point. If your wrist is bent upward (cupped), the clubface is closed, and if you don't make any adjustment, you're going to hit the ball left. If the wrist is bent downward (bowed), the clubface is open, and you'll hit the ball right unless you do something like turn really hard. So, obviously, the way to hit straighter shots is to try to get that wrist flat at the top of the backswing. I like to think of it as lifting my left hand up in a fist and pounding it on a little table that's sitting in front of my left thigh. You wouldn't pound on that table with your wrist cupped or bowed. You'd have it flat and stable, so you could deliver the most power to the table and do the least damage to your wrist.

Even if you tame your slice back into a reliable fade—or even into a draw—you have to pay attention to your position in the tee box. When I tee it up with my amateur partners in pro-ams, I see more guys than I can count just walk up and hit from the middle of the box, without even thinking about it. If all you ever hit is a straight ball, that'd be fine. For the rest of us who curve it one way or another, it always makes sense to move to one side of the tee box or the other. In the next chapter, I'll tell you more about coming up with a good tee box strategy to suit the way you hit the ball.

5

STRATEGY

Probably the biggest misconception about the sport of long driving is that we get up there and swing mindlessly, hoping to get lucky and catch one that lands on the grid. That's definitely not true for me, and it shouldn't be for you when you stand over your tee shot.

On both the long-drive tee box and the tee of your course at home, the goal is the same—have a plan for what you want to do and set yourself up the right way to do it, then let it go and swing without trying to steer it. What does that mean? Let me start by telling you how it works at the World Championship.

The first thing I do when I get to Mesquite is go out to where the grid is set up, at the end of the driving range at the Palms Golf Course. There's a gravel access road that runs down the side of the grid, and I drive right out to the end and get out. I walk out on the grass and work my way back and forth on the grid between the 350 and 380 signs, because that's where my shots are probably going to land. I'm testing the ground with my feet, feeling to see if it is spongy or firm, and which side of the grid is more receptive to a shot rolling after it lands. The condition of the grid tells me if I'm going to have to hit a higher launching shot or play a shot that rolls more.

In the finals of the 2001 championship, the fastest parts of the grid were on the edges where maintenance carts had been driving on the grass—pretty close to the out-of-bounds stripes. I moved over toward the right middle of the tee box, aimed for the right center of the grid, and played for a slight draw. If I turned it over to the left a bit too much, I knew I was going to have a good chance to win, because that's where all the longest balls come from—slight pulls. But from that spot in the tee box, I also knew that if I didn't turn it over at all I'd still be in the grid.

It might look like we're out there banging away, just hoping one of them comes down on the grid, but there's definitely strategy and planning that goes into it. And I'm sure the people who own houses down the right side of some of the holes back home at Chenal Country Club in Little Rock are glad that I'm doing my best to take their kitchen windows out of play.

At the 2005 championship, everybody was talking about how fast and firm it was going to be, but I had been checking the weather for a month leading up to the event, and I knew the Mesquite area had gotten a lot of rain. When I went out and checked the grid early in the week, it confirmed what I had seen in the weather reports. It was soggy. I had been practicing my high shots for the last two weeks, and I was ready for the tournament. Other guys had to scramble around and switch to more lofted drivers, and they didn't have as much time to prepare. When I got to the finals, all I was thinking about was swinging my club. I wasn't worried about my equipment setup, or about trying to hit it high under all that pressure. It was a tremendous advantage. My winning drive in 2005 rolled one yard after it landed. In 1995, I found the firmer part of the grid and my shot rolled 42 yards. You've got to have a variety of shots in your arsenal so you can take advantage of different conditions.

Now, I don't want to give the impression that I'm picking a spot on the ground and aiming for that when I hit my shots in competition. When I'm really on, I can be that specific with where I'm aiming. Mostly what I'm doing is figuring out the side of the grid I want to favor, just like you would for the fairway at your course. When it comes to aiming, I like to pick a landmark in the distance, like one of the telephone poles that line the expressway behind the grid in Mesquite. Then I can visualize my shot never leaving the line of that pole on its way down the range.

They've done a great job at the championship making the grid more consistent. In 1997 and 1998, I hit balls that I knew were plenty hard enough to win, but they landed soft and checked up when I expected them to roll. Of course, every long driver has been on both sides of that, getting a good bounce to advance or a bad bounce that sends you home. It's part of the game. But it's easier to deal with now that there's a higher standard of maintenance on the grid as a whole.

I'm certainly not the only guy to go scout out the grid to get a sense for where I want to hit my shots. But I think a lot of guys who go with the intent of finding the right place to hit it still don't get the benefit of doing that research because they don't have the ability to hit a different kind of shot under pressure. Being able to stand up there knowing you need a high ball and being able to hit it with all those people watching is the real test in the sport.

The inexperienced long driver is making a lot of the same mistakes on the grid as the average amateur does when he's playing a round at home. A rookie long driver goes up there and tries to hit it too hard. He's competing against the other guys in his group, not trying to simply make his best swing and see what happens. That's true about the average player, too. When your opponent in a match-play situation gets up there and bombs one, your impulse is to go at it harder to try to match that shot. The better play is to fake yourself out. Really. I convince myself that I'm really back home hitting balls at Chenal, and all I have to do is make my swing. When you're relaxed and loose and feeling like you're swinging at 85 percent, that's when you're going to hit some great shots under pressure.

The opposite side of that problem is the tendency to try to guide it. At the World Championship, you see it when a guy keeps missing shots short and right, or his arms slow down and his hands get overactive and turn the club over. He's trying *too* hard to gear it down and get one into play, and he's not releasing the club aggressively and naturally through impact.

For the average amateur player, guiding it comes from the complete disconnect most players have between practicing at the range and actually playing golf. Ask yourself if this sounds familiar. When you're at the range, you think about mechanics and balance, and you get into a rhythm of hitting balls. Tee it up. Check grip. Get a good feel. Let it go. The major thing missing from that is a target. At most, you're looking out to see your ball flight—whether the ball is curving left or right, or how far you hit it.

The problem is, when you get out on the course and stand on the tee, you see things like out-of-bounds stakes, creeks, and ponds. You know that there's a penalty—a bad score—if you don't hit this one particular shot well. On the course, your mind is dealing with a whole different set of variables. That's where the problems come in. You're trying to do something your body isn't used to doing. Add in the pressure of a few bucks on the line, or a particularly scary shot with trouble all around, and it's no wonder so many players struggle to get off the tee.

"Swing like you're on the driving range" is good advice as far as tempo goes, but it's really incomplete. I want you to swing like you do on the driving range, but change your driving range practice technique so that you're aiming at a specific target for every shot you hit. That helps you square yourself up to where you want to hit it, which by itself is a huge improvement over what most people do. You can pick anything out there toward the end of the range—a flag or one of the posts holding the nets up, for example. Just be sure to pick a specific target every time.

If you look at the average tee box, you've got about 10 yards of space between the markers to set up for your shot. I wish I had a dollar for every guy in my pro-am group who walks up and sticks the tee in the ground in the middle somewhere, then aims down the middle and hits the same fade he's had for thirty years into the right rough.

If you hit a fade from left to right, you can dramatically increase your chances of hitting the fairway by moving to the far right of the tee box and aiming for the left edge of the fairway. If you pull it, you're in the left rough. A straight shot puts you on the left side of the fairway. And you've got the entire width of the fairway to play your fade—twice as much as you would have if you had aimed down the middle. If you hit a draw from right to left, you'd do the opposite—tee it up on the left side and aim for the right edge of the fairway. When you pick your target, make sure that a straight ball won't get you in trouble. Aiming for the middle of a pond and waiting for it to curve back into play is a little more stress than I like to experience.

I set up to the right side of the tee both when I'm playing and when I'm competing, because I know I'm prone to pushing shots out to the right. From the right side of the tee box, I've got so much more room for error. Aiming just left of center, I can hit a little pull, a straight ball, or a little fade and still be in good shape. I'm aiming back across the fattest part of the fairway instead of cutting off half my landing area by hitting from the middle of the tee and aiming at the middle.

Sometimes, when I'm hitting a consistent pull, I'll aim down the right side and try to pull the ball back on the grid, but that's risky. For me, a pull is really close to a good shot, and if I really catch one, I'll hit some mammoth shots dead straight, and they'll flirt with the right out-of-bounds line. I've lost at least two championships when deep, deep drives trickled out just right of the grid by a yard or two on shots like that.

The way you hold the club has a huge impact on how you set up, and, in turn, where your shots go. Because you hold the club with your right hand below your left, the tendency is to open your shoulders to make it easier for your lower arm to reach the lower point of the grip. It just feels better to set up this way. But open shoulders will tend to make you hit across the ball and curve it to the right. Set up to your tee shot, then hold your driver across your chest at mid-shoulder height. You'll probably see that club pointing left of where you thought you were aiming. To fix this open shoulder problem, simply tilt your spine away from the target a little more—in other words, lower your right shoulder. This will help your right arm get in a more comfortable position without your shoulders having to open up.

If your shoulders are open to your target line, or if your feet are open and your shoulders are square, you need to be as far over on the right side of the tee box as you can get. Only players who consistently draw the ball should be anywhere near the left side of the tee box, for the same reasons we just talked about. With a draw, you want to set up on the left, aim for the right side of the fairway, and give yourself that margin for error on both sides.

Once you start taking more care in where you set up in the tee box and how you actually aim yourself, you'll be amazed at how much more freely you can swing at the ball. I'm convinced that a lot of the indecision and steering of the ball that comes with a bad driving game is from a lack of confidence in where you're aiming, not because of any specific swing flaw. You can play decent golf with just about any kind of ball flight—especially if it's consistent—if you know how to align yourself to take the best advantage of that flight.

One question I get a lot is about hazards down one side of a hole or another. A lot of players want to know if it's a better play to take something shorter off the tee and make sure you get it in the fairway. I think that's a bad strategy unless there's trouble on *both* sides of the fairway. I've said it before and I'll say it again. Personally, I'd rather be in the woods 350 yards from the tee in one shot than in the woods 250 yards from the tee in one. If you're 50 yards from the green, you can punch out and still make par.

If you're standing there at the toughest hole on your course— you know, that uphill 430-yard par-4 with out-of-bounds all the way down the right side—you want to make a positive plan for your shot, not play defense against the shot you don't want to hit. I like the guy who sees that tee shot and says to himself, "I've got a shot for that. I'm going to aim for that left rough and hit my reliable fade out there. No problem." The guy who gets himself in trouble (or into the backyard of that house over there) is the one who decides to try to hit a big hook away from the trouble, or makes a tentative swing to try to bunt it out there.

I know saying it is easy but doing it is hard, but if the only thing you take from this is the idea that you want to do everything related to your tee shot with specific intention, you're going to have a lot more success—even if you don't change a single thing about your swing. Just having a specific, positive intention simplifies your swing thoughts and lets your body do the automatic, muscle-memory thing it wants to do. Even if that's a 210-yard ball with 20 yards of slice, that's fine—if you play for it.

The distance commandments I talked about in chapter 3 are really going to help you when it comes to strategy because they let you be more aggressive with both your mind-set and your swing. If you're feeling better about swinging the club harder and more confident that the ball is going to go more toward where you planned for it to go, you're going to be able to let it go and actually swing at it, as opposed to hitting and hoping.

I'm not a big fan of playing conservatively off the tee. Laying up with an iron on a par-4 is basically conceding that you're not going to hit the green with your second shot. First, if you hit your driver so badly that you don't think there's much of a chance of finding your shot, that club shouldn't even be in your bag. The only time I'm in favor of hitting something other than driver is when it doesn't make any sense to try to hit it longer. If the fairway runs out at 220 yards and you hit your driver 230, then hitting five-wood is obviously a better option. If you're playing a 300-yard par-4 and all the bunkers start 50 yards from the green, it doesn't make much sense to bomb a driver down there *unless* you can hit it 300 yards and you're a good bunker player. I know I'd rather be in a greenside bunker than standing over a 50-yard wedge shot. I hit my 66-degree club 110 yards, so it's hard for me to dial it down that short.

I know what you're thinking: "Hit driver all the time? That's easy for you to say. You've never seen me hit my bad ones." Actually, yes, I have. And I know that the average 90-shooter is capable of hitting bad shots with any club in the bag. I believe a 90-shooter is better off hitting driver from most tees because the misses are going to be just as bad with that club as with any other, but the good shots are going to give him so much more advantage. I also think that hitting driver more often gives you more familiarity with the club. Instead of it being some alien thing that you only swing two or three times during a round because you're afraid of what might happen, it becomes a club that you've actually hit some good shots with. And remembering the good shots you hit and applying those memories to new situations in front of you is a powerful way to overcome nervousness on the tee—whether you're on the grid in front of 4,000 people or playing against a buddy you just can't seem to beat.

For me, if I'm trying to rip it down the right side with a little draw, I just think about my favorite hole at Chenal, number 9. I've hit that shot a million times there, so I know I've got it in me. I went from a 20-handicapper to a five in the span of about a year mostly by using visualization techniques like that on the tee—not by getting a bunch of lessons on my swing. Watch me hit it a five-iron and you won't confuse me with a PGA Tour player. But I shoot rounds in the low 70s more often than not. It's amazing what can happen when you just decide to visualize and attack your shots instead of playing defensively. (I'm going to talk a lot more about visualization in chapter 6.)

There's another entire component to tee shot strategy that most people don't even think of. I actually build four different clubhead-shaft combinations to play specific kinds of wind and ground conditions at the World Championship. I have a tailwind/hardpan club, a tailwind/soft club, a headwind/hardpan club, and a headwind/soft club. With a tailwind, I want to hit it higher with less backspin on hardpan, and harder with more backspin on soft conditions. Into a headwind, I want low trajectory and low spin on hard conditions, and all the carry and backspin I can get on soft conditions. By using a club with a little less loft and a shaft that's more flexible, I can hit it lower with more spin. More loft and a stiffer shaft produces shots that fly higher and spin less, and so on. On the higher-launch clubs, the ball is going out at 16 degrees, while the lower-launch clubs send it out at 12 degrees. You can really tell the difference when you're standing behind me and watching. I always bring copies of each of those four different kinds clubs to the World Championship so I'm ready for whatever conditions I find when I get there. One year, I even named all the clubs after *Andy Griffith* characters. Before you even ask, no, I didn't name any of them Aunt Bea. (I had an Opie, an Andy, a Gomer, a Goober, and a Barney. Barney ended up being the best one.)

Telling you to go out and buy a bunch of different drivers for the conditions and situations you face at your course might be a bit extreme, but I don't think it's crazy to have two different drivers in your arsenal, built with different specs. If you're playing a shorter course that places more of a premium on accuracy, it makes sense to have a driver with a little more loft and a shaft maybe an inch shorter than standard. That club would also work well on a day when the ground is softer and you need carry more than roll. On courses with more room and longer holes, you could have a driver with less loft and a shaft that might even be an inch longer than standard. You'd be able to give up a little accuracy to get the added benefit of more distance, without too much risk. That would be a fantastic driver to take with you to St. Andrews, to play in the wind and on the hard ground Scotland has in the summertime.

What happens when wind conditions change throughout your round? You can make some slight adjustments to your setup and swing to account for the wind either blowing into you or with you.

If the wind is helping, tilt your spine a little bit more away from the target by slightly lowering your right shoulder. This will help you catch the ball more on the upswing and launch it higher in the air, taking advantage of the wind. Into a headwind, you do the opposite: lower your left shoulder to get your shoulders more square to the ground, to hit a more penetrating, running shot. An easy way to check this is to hold a club up to the front of your shoulders and see where the shaft is pointing. This is a good indicator of your shot trajectory off the face of the club.

PREPARATION

There's a reason two guys who aren't the biggest or strongest hitters in the sport have won eight of the last twelve world titles. It's because the week of the World Championship is just the end result of fifty-one other weeks of physical and mental preparation that go into being world-class at anything—whether it's long driving, basketball, or tennis.

Jason Zuback is listed at 5 foot 10 (and that's probably a little generous), but he works out relentlessly and is as prepared mentally and physically as any athlete I've ever seen. There's a reason he's won five world championships, and why I respect him more than any other long driver. I think he and I succeed where other guys have more trouble because we're committed to being prepared for the biggest event in our sport, and we both prepare the right way.

I don't know exactly what Jason's training regimen is, but I know that when I talk to him about some of the cutting-edge training and visualization techniques I'm working on, he's always very familiar with them. Rob Tillman, my physical therapist, introduced me to ballistic exercises—using a pulley system with sliding weights for resistance—that make me fire my fast-twitch muscles. In 2000, I told Jason about the workout, and he'd already been doing the same kinds of things. He's the only other person in our sport I've talked to who had been training that way

My taste for physical and mental preparation goes all the way back to college at Florida, under Coach Bozeman. He told us we couldn't control whether other schools had better or stronger athletes. But if we didn't do everything in our power to be physically and mentally ready to compete, and to get the most out of the abilities we had, we were wasting our time.

The psychology of being prepared is powerful, too. If you can go into a big event knowing you've done everything you can to be ready—from training to hitting balls to getting your equipment dialed in—there's some peace that comes with that. You know you're ready to give your best effort, and if you aren't successful it'll be because somebody else was simply better that day. That feeling is so much better than self-doubt—"Did I do enough?" or "Am I ready?" I've been in both boats, believe me.

I break my preparation for the World Championship into three distinct segments—three trimesters in the year, basically. The first segment, which is the four months directly after the World Championship, is dedicated to working out and building a good strong base of strength and conditioning. The second segment is all about getting into "hitting shape," which I'll describe a little more in a second. The third segment is about maintaining myself physically and working on mental routine and preparation.

Even if you don't break your own golf season down as specifically as I do, I know you'll benefit from incorporating some of the elements of my preparation plan into your routine.

Physical Training

I'm always mentally fried and physically wiped out by the end of the World Championship week in the fall. When you're a top-tier long driver, you're doing a hundred gigs a year at courses and ranges all over the world. There's advantages to that—you're hitting in front of people and doing interviews, so you're not nervous in front of the camera—but after winning in 2005, I didn't have time to practice or train like I wanted to for the next season. Leading up to the 2006 championship, I was in Taiwan, Malaysia, the Philippines, Singapore, China, and Japan in the month before the event. I had nothing left in the tank when I got home, and I had a slightly torn rotator cuff and a torn wrist tendon, too. So when other guys were doing what I usually do—beat balls and practice—I was wearing myself out on the plane and in exhibition contests across Asia. That's a mistake I won't make again.

In a typical year, when the championship is over and I'm ready to start the process all over again, I immediately hit the weight room with my trainer, Robert Farqua of Arkansas Fitness in Little Rock. I met Robert through Rob Tillman, my physical therapist, and using Robert is some of the best advice I've ever gotten.

Robert is a bastard, and I mean that in the nicest possible way. He's as tough as you can imagine—a former amateur boxer who has trained ultimate fighters to have enough endurance to be able to get kicked and punched in the head over and over. He's just an all-around badass. I respond to that kind of guy—one who won't let me get away with anything. I can be sick in bed and get a call from Robert, and he'll tell me to get my ass down to the gym and work out for at least a half hour.

For five months, Robert and I will hit it hard in the gym, doing a series of exercises specifically designed to build fast-twitch muscle fibers—which in turn builds clubhead and ball speed. The secret to Robert's technique is that he gets me doing a variety of exercises, like military presses or dips between weight benches, up until failure. Using the bench dips as an example, I'll do them until I can't go anymore, then take a 60-second rest on the bench. Then I go again with the dips until I can't go anymore, then repeat the process. By the third cycle, my bigger slow-twitch muscles are fried, and the fast-twitch fibers get recruited to help out. Or I'll stand with my arms held straight out with five-pound weights in each hand. I have to twirl the plates in small circles with my arms for three minutes, then rest for a minute, then do it again for three minutes. Think that's easy? Try it. It'll crush you the first time.

What you're doing is finding your failure point and trying to constantly push it farther away from you with each workout. Many people have no idea where their muscle failure point is because they've never reached it. You'll be surprised how far you can go if you push yourself. A trainer can be there to help you and motivate you, and Robert does a great, no-nonsense job at that. He deals only with people who have a professional attitude about training, and he'll fire you as a client if you don't come in that way. Let's put it this way: at his gym there aren't any people standing around the machines chatting each other up for dates.

All I have to do is watch the DVDs of the 2000 and 2001 World Championships to reinforce how valuable Robert's advice and motivation is to me. In 2000, I came in at a sloppy 256 pounds and finished tenth. After eight months of Robert's training and nutrition program, I came into the 2001 championship at 220 pounds. I was lighter and stronger, and I became the oldest man to win the championship, at age thirty-nine.

You're probably wondering, is hitting it longer simply about working out in the gym and building a bunch of big muscles? No, not exactly. There are specific muscle groups you should be focusing on to get "golf strong," as opposed to "gym strong." For a long time, the conventional wisdom in golf was that you didn't want to use weights to get fit because you didn't want to get muscle-bound. Johnny Miller said he lost his game because he spent a winter clearing trees from his property and bulked up too much.

Take one look at Tiger Woods—or Zuback, for that matter— and you'll quickly see that the idea you shouldn't work out with weights as a golfer is crazy. Doing the right kind of strength training is absolutely critical to competing at the top level of both conventional golf and long driving. If it weren't for strength training under Robert's guidance, I have no doubt I wouldn't have won two of my three titles, and I'm sure I'd be sitting at some desk job by now, in my mid-forties, instead of continuing to compete.

What muscles do you want to develop to get more distance? The shoulder girdle is huge. It's the ring of muscle that crosses around the back, just below your shoulder blades, and extends under your arm and around to your pectoral muscle on the front of your chest. Your left tricep also plays a big part, along with the inner tricep on your right arm and your right bicep. The true mark of a power swinger is the muscle on the top of the forearm. That's the one that provides the snap at impact, or whips the bat through the hitting zone.

For stability, you want to start with inner-thigh exercises, stretching an elastic band around your ankles and doing crossovers with both legs. "Core strength" is a hot new phrase PGA Tour golfers are using these days. It's nice that they could catch up. Long drivers have been working on core strength for more than ten years—developing the obliques and abdominals. Those muscles are responsible for your torso rotation back and through, and the way your hips uncoil and explode through the ball.

In addition to working on presses, dips, and other explosive moves with weights to build strength, I'll hit a heavy bag with a softball bat to recruit the muscle groups that are responsible for swinging a golf club. Another way to do that is to hold a medicine ball at waist height in front of you, stand sideways, and chuck the ball down the line to a partner 10 feet away. This builds up the muscles in your back and sides and makes the club feel incredibly light. I also like to use the cable pull-down machine, holding the grips like I would a golf club and simulating my downswing with 200 pounds of weight on the rack.

You wouldn't think that cardio work would be important for a long driver—after all, we're not walking 18 holes, like Tour players do. But I've found that good cardio is the key to the stamina I need to hit hundreds of balls in high-pressure situations at the championship. It helps me keep my breathing relaxed under that pressure, and my legs feel as good at the end of the night on Sunday as they did when I showed up to hit my first practice ball the previous Monday. I start every workout with a three-mile ride on the stationary bike, which I have to complete in less than 10 minutes. It gets my blood pumping and my metabolism working before the heavyweight stuff comes next.

I'm not a big believer in training aids, but one I use every day is the Momentus Power Hitter. The Power Hitter is a hittable driver that's built with extra weight in the head and shaft (so the swingweight is balanced and close to that of a regular driver). The 310 model is twice as heavy as a standard driver, and it forces you to swing on plane, with a smooth transition at the top. The weight helps you stretch and make a bigger turn, and it builds the muscles that help you hit the ball longer. I'll warm up with the Power

Hitter for 20 or 30 shots, and when I switch out to my regular driver, it feels light and fast. It also helps me a lot with my push and slice. You can't cast with it and throw your shoulder over the top, so you start swinging it from the inside.

One question I get a lot is about stretching, and which stretches are good to do before a round. The truth is, I don't stretch. I'm one of the least flexible guys around, and I don't think a stretching regimen would change that fact. I've also had a lot of back problems, and I try to be as careful as I can about putting my back through any extra twisting and turning. I concentrate on getting warm and avoiding muscle pulls by hitting balls with a heavy club. That's my stretching routine. Rob Tillman told me that stretching would cause my muscles to contract more slowly—something I don't want when I'm trying to hit a long ball.

My swing is about power, explosiveness, and muscle strength, for sure, but I watch with some jealousy my buddy John Daly swing. I wish I could get as much shoulder turn as he has. If I could get that length in my backswing, I'd pick up 30 yards. When John won the PGA Championship in 1991, I went out that day and tried to copy his swing. I couldn't even hit the ball. He can turn that way and keep his left arm straight, which is amazing. I have to rely on my hand speed.

All that being said, I do think that the average player—who doesn't have my physical limitations in terms of a back injury—could benefit from doing some specific stretches. That's especially true given that you aren't going to have the same kind of hand speed I do. I've been on a machine that measures your "X factor"—the amount your shoulders turn relative to your hips at the top of your backswing. The average tour player has a differential of 40 or 45 degrees. My turn is 17 degrees. Being able to get more coil is one way to generate a lot more power. I do it more with hand speed, like I said, but if you can increase this X factor—in addition to improving your technique in the ways I've been describing—you'll hit the ball farther. The key muscle group to stretch to improve your X factor is the band of muscles around the outside of your hips. Those hip flexors are what allow you to turn like that—and more important, turn while keeping your hips relatively square to the target line.

One way to get more flexibility in that area is to lie down on the ground like you are going to make some snow angels. Start by pulling one knee up to your chest, then crossing it over your other leg and touching the ground next to you with it. Alternate and do the same thing with your other knee, holding it on the ground for a count of ten. Then pull both knees up to your chest and turn your lower body while keeping your shoulders flat against the floor. You should feel a stretch down your side and along the side of your hip when you do this. If you don't, you're not turning far enough.

I also like to do some gentle stretches when I'm done playing, just to cool down my muscles and get blood circulating through them. I'll shrug my shoulders and rotate them forward and then bend at the waist, gently touching my toes and shaking my hands a little bit. The goal isn't so much to improve flexibility as to move some of the lactic acid that builds up after using your muscles. I'm also a big believer in cold packs versus heat when it comes to treating sore muscles after a workout or a round. I carry a bag with me to every event that has a set of wraps and braces and gel packs that I can put in the refrigerator or a freezer. I come back to the room, stick one of the packs into the back strap, wrap it around me, and relax until my muscles loosen. Advil (ibuprofen) also works great because it is an anti-inflammatory.

Hitting Shape

There's definitely a difference between being in good physical shape and being in hitting shape. It's the same for a baseball player who trains all winter but still needs spring training to see some pitches and shake off the game rust. The hitting shape part of my program is where I accomplish three things: improving my swing mechanics, sorting out the equipment that I'm going to be using at the championship, and building up my swinging stamina.

Every day, I go over to the ninth tee at Chenal and hit drives from 7 a.m. until the first group makes the turn, at 9:15. Then I'll go to the range and hit another 90 minutes before I take a break for lunch. I'll hit balls all afternoon, too. I used to hit as many as a thousand a day, but now that number is about three hundred because my body just can't take that kind of pounding anymore.

Have you ever hit so many balls that your muscles become fatigued and you start hitting the ball shorter instead of longer? The purpose of being in hitting shape is so that when I get to the championship, I don't have to be concerned about whether I've got enough left by the time the finals come around. I don't have to conserve energy or save anything. By the time I get to Mesquite, I'm actually hitting far *fewer* balls per day in the actual competition than I was during practice. It almost feels like a vacation.

It's during my swing training period that I'm working on things like hitting the ball higher or lower. I'll hit hundreds of balls play-ing a high draw, and hundreds playing a low straight shot. I want those shots to be second nature in Mesquite. I just want to think it and do it. The only way for that to happen is to take all the drama out of it by putting the practice time in.

I wish I could give you some secret piece of advice that would make it so you didn't have to work on your game, but the fact is, if you want your handicap to go down significantly, you're going to have to practice more often than you play. And it isn't even so much to work on "new" swing advice. As long as you practice with a target and a goal for each session, the process of hitting a large bucket of balls will improve your sense for how the ball is coming off the club. You'll be able to better predict what your shots are going to do on the golf course—and that isn't dependent on being able to hit them longer or straighter than you did before.

Before you start your next golf season, try going to the range at least ten times before you play your first round of golf. Go with a real plan for your golf swing—using this book is a good way to do it—and shake the rust off under practice conditions instead of on the first tee for your first round of the spring. Not only will you have a better handle on the game you're coming to the course with, but you'll be in better hitting shape. You'll have more flexibility, and your muscles will be ready to play 18 holes. You already know I'm a big believer in confidence. I think if you start your season that way, at full speed, you'll be able to build on better performances earlier in the season, and your peak will be higher. I know there have been seasons here in Little Rock where I felt like I was just getting into the groove of playing well when the good weather ran out on me. Push that groove back a month and you can really have some fun.

Mental Preparation

My mental preparation techniques might come up last in terms of how this chapter is organized and where they fit in the sequence of what I do to prepare for the championship, but they're the most important things I do to get ready to hit a ball as far as I can.

In long driving, a lot of guys have the physical tools to hit the ball far. The only way to separate yourself from the pack is to be able to deal with your emotions better and compete at a level closest to your optimum ability even when the pressure is at its greatest. The secret to competing is to do everything the same way you always do. You're reinforcing to your mind and body that you're not doing anything out of the ordinary. If you try to eat something especially nutritious for the big occasion or go to bed early, you're sending all kinds of bad signals to your subconscious. I make a point of wearing the same shirts and pants, watching the same shows on TV, and so on, that I normally do. You've got to tell your mind and body that it's just another day at the office.

One advantage I have is being a former athlete in college. I've competed, and I've competed in front of crowds. I can tune those distractions out pretty easily, and that's definitely part of the battle. Some guys just can't deal with the hollering and the lights that come with getting to the final group of six. If you came up through junior or college golf, you've never played in front of people. Even mini-tour players who have seen galleries have never been exposed to the atmosphere at the World Championship, where people are yelling as if it were a boxing match. My first year in front of that crowd, I set up to my ball and my hamstrings were shaking so bad I couldn't even take the club back. I knew I was done before I even swung.

When you get under the gun like that, your body is releasing adrenaline—for fight or flight. The more you're in that position, the more you get used to that shot of adrenaline. Personally, I thrive on it now, to the point where it hurts me in earlier rounds. When I get cranked up on that adrenaline rush, my clubhead speed picks up by eight or nine miles per hour. Earlier in the tournament week, when I'm hitting in front of empty bleachers, it's hard to get myself as charged up. I've gone out early a couple of times, losing to be guys who shouldn't have beaten me, because I couldn't flip that switch.

Still, my record once I get to the finals is one of the best in the business, and I firmly believe it's because of my practice routines during the year and my visualization techniques. When I get to the final round, I believe I'm going to win.

When I practice, everything I do is geared toward making what I see on the practice tee the same as it'll be when I'm competing. I'll hit six balls, just like we do in the championship. I'll divide those six balls into two groups of three, just like I do at the championship. I'll even set up scenarios for myself—that I've got no balls in the grid and I need the last one to be long and good, things like that. I want to be intensely focused. You have to harness the rage and aggression a little bit, instead of thinking about flailing away as hard as you can. I'm trying to be fluid and violent at the same time. The way that happens is by swinging the club as hard as I can at first, getting my clubhead speed up to the mid-150s, then backing up to about 85 percent of that. That's where you find those extra 20 yards, by being aggressive right up to your 85 percent speed.

One of my favorite ways to add some consequences to my practice routine is to play "move the towel." I'll get out on the ninth hole at Chenal. I'll hit six balls, then drive down and chart where they landed (I'm constantly trying to keep my average up to three in the fairway for every six I hit). The towel goes out in the fairway on the spot where my longest ball ends up. You're constantly trying to move the towel out for the length of the practice session. I'll be out there hitting for three hours, and for two and a half of them it's pretty easy to consistently edge that towel out to about 370. At the end of my session, I'll tell myself I've got six balls left and I've got to move the towel or I'm going home without the trophy. And I have to say that there are a lot of times when I'll move that towel on my last six.

This game came from my time as a discus thrower in college. The team would practice together, and you always wanted to be the guy who owned the towel, because it meant you had the longest throw.

This next part might sound a little bit out there, but I'm convinced visualization works. And it's not just me. Zuback has his own routine, and an overwhelmingly high percentage of pro athletes from other sports that I've played with or talked to say they use some sort of visualization technique.

The first time I was introduced to visualization was when I was pole-vaulting in the tenth grade. My mom was telling her boss at the real estate company she worked for about how bad my vaulting was. He had been using some hypnotism and visualization techniques to improve his selling skills, and he invited me over to his office and showed me how to do it. I'd lie down and totally relax in a dark room before I vaulted—and picture myself making good vaults. The next year I came back and broke the school record.

Later on, I met a hypnotherapist, Dr. Jerry Jacobsen, who made me a set of audiotapes to reinforce what I was doing. I developed a mental routine to go through every time I got ready to compete. When I lived in Georgia as a kid, we had a well in our yard that we took baths next to. I visualize going down the well, and once I get to the bottom, I walk through a musty area into a mall-like area, then down an escalator and down ten stairs. I open this big iron door, then lock it. I open another door, then go into this small room and put a big bar on the door. I lie down on a sheet and pillow that are in the middle of the room and close my eyes. I relax my entire

Before I hit any shot in competition, I go through my visualization routine and see the trajectory I want, along with the positive result. It helps me block out all the distractions around me.

body, part by part, and when I'm fully relaxed, I go through the visualization. I see my ball flight, and see myself hitting it pure. I see myself hitting sets of six balls in a row just perfect, then see myself winning the trophy and giving my speech. Once I do that, I retrace my steps and climb back out of the well. When I get back up to the top, after about 30 minutes, I'm a totally different person. Seriously.

I have a tape of the hypnotherapist going through the journey I just described, step by step. I listen to that tape two or three times a day for the two months leading up to the World Championship. It takes 26 minutes to listen to it and find that zone of total concentration. In 2001, I was down to my last ball. Standing behind

Once I visualize what I want to do and step into my stance, I'm not thinking anything technical, like swing mechanics. I'm looking for my aiming point in the distance and thinking about my ball never leaving that line.

that shot, I closed my eyes, got in that little room at high speed, and saw my ball flight two or three times. After that, I just went up and executed. The shot I hit perfectly matched the mental imagery in my head. I wouldn't believe it if it hadn't happened to me. But I'm definitely a believer, and I know guys like Zuback—and Tiger Woods—do it.

Hey, I'm not trying to tell you to stand up on the tee and think happy thoughts, or to look out at a water hazard and pretend it isn't there. When I hear sports psychologists talking that way and over-simplifying things, it turns me off pretty fast. Because if the first time you're trying to calm yourself down and visualize something positive is when you're on the tee looking at that water hazard, it's too late. Just like anything else in your golf game, you need to practice it so it's there when you need it.

The best way to get started with visualization is to go to the range and hit balls. You need to experiment with visualizing the flight of your shots before you hit them. Try picturing yourself as if you're watching yourself hit a shot on a TV broadcast, including the cutaway to the ball in flight, going right at the target. That's easy for some people to do and hard for others. If it's easy for you, that's a good key to use for your visualization.

Some people can lock onto a feel more easily than a picture of a ball flight. If you're one of those players, you want to lock in what it feels like to hit it solid, or maybe what it feels like to make a complete turn in the backswing. For me, when I catch one absolutely pure, it feels like a whiff, like the ball wasn't even there. You want to hit shots on the range and essentially "record" in your head what the feels were for the good ones. You know how a certain song or smell reminds you of a good time you once had? Recalling those feels works in the same sort of way.

I know of some players who use a swing key or thought as part of that visualization. Essentially, they're locking on one particular swing thought—like keeping the backswing low and slow—and using that one thought to block out any other distractions. I haven't found too many good players who say they just go completely blank during a swing. That makes me believe that you're going to be thinking *something*, so you should probably have a plan for what you want it to be, so it can be a productive thought.

For me, the visualization part of my routine has really been effective because it gets me "away" from all the noise and activity and stress that comes with competing. I'm able to focus on one thing— my performance—when I'm getting ready to compete. Going away from it all, down those steps, gets me away from crowd noise, distractions from other competitors—even the normal thoughts that come with everyday life like mortgage payments and the kids' bumps and bruises. I've found that when I'm easily distracted—say, when I'm really tired—it's also really easy for negative thoughts and doubts to creep in. By concentrating on one thing, it's almost like you're tricking your brain into forgetting about the nervousness.

One thing I want you to remember is that everybody makes mental mistakes—and I mean everybody. The way you get better is by learning from them. You're going to get discouraged from time to time after a particularly bad one. That's natural, and it's a good thing, because it means you care about what you're doing out there. But when you make one of those mistakes, you've got to move on from it and learn.

I've made so many mental mistakes over the years—overswinging, going up there feeling like I have to murder it. In 1998, I was swinging faster than I've ever done, but that was actually too hard for the shafts in my clubs. When I was training for the championship, I knew I was going to be swinging harder when the adrenaline was flowing, but I didn't account for how *much* harder when I was planning out what shaft flex to use. I got to the semifinals and was so out of control that I couldn't make solid contact. I knew what was happening, but I couldn't stop it. I couldn't get the club to do what I wanted, and I didn't think about just swinging at 85 percent (like we talked about in chapter 4).

Another mistake came the year after I won my first title. I thought I had a cakewalk to the final round. I looked at my draw and didn't see any names I recognized. I even told my wife I had it made. In the second round, I got eliminated by two guys who ended up in the finals—Zuback, who won, and Carl Hasselback, who finished second. At the time, I definitely didn't love going home early that way, but getting burned like that made me pay much closer attention the next time. Having it happen to me early in my World Championship career was definitely an overall positive.

Working out these preparation routines was a lot like coming up with my Long-Drive Bible. I made a lot of mistakes and wrote down and incorporated the things that worked into my process for being successful. I hope to save you some of that time—and pain—and give you some shortcuts.

I said before that this book wasn't designed to turn you into a competitive long driver, but I know some guys who are trying to get into the sport will take this information and use it as ammunition when they compete against me. I'm not real comfortable with that, but in the end, if somebody wins a word title with my help, that's a good thing.

7

EQUIPMENT

There's been so much talk about dramatic improvements in driver technology over the last ten years that it's almost a cliché now. But when you look at video from the first championship I won, in 1995, and compare it to the 2005 championship, it's like we're playing different sports (and I don't want to hear any jokes about the cheesy shirts we were wearing back then).

In 1995, I used a TaylorMade Pittsburgh Persimmon model clubhead. It was made out of steel and was, at most, 185 cubic centimeters in size. New drivers go right up to the USGA maximum of 460 cc—almost three times as big. That Pittsburgh Persimmon looks like one of today's seven-woods, except it wasn't nearly as easy to hit. Take a look at the face of your fairway wood and compare it to the face of your driver and you'll get an idea of the difference in terms of forgiveness. Those old straight-faced metal woods look like they aren't much wider than the ball itself. I don't know if it was any harder for us to hit them solid then compared to now, because we didn't know any better, but if you missed the sweet spot on the old driver, you were done because the ball wasn't going anywhere. On a new driver, the average guy can miss the center of the face by an inch—which is a lot—and still hit one decent.

The first oversize drivers I saw in the mid-1990s were 340 cc and made out of steel. I tried them out, but the faces dented really quickly—like after two or three balls. I also heard a really loud whoosh when the club came through impact, which made me feel like I was losing some clubhead speed because of wind resistance. What it came down to was that I just didn't get much more distance with that first generation of oversize clubs, so I stuck with my old clubs.

Titanium changed everything, though. Clubheads could be made bigger and lighter than those made from steel, and titanium is 30 percent stronger as well. Because clubs could be made so light, the size of the club (and the increased wind resistance) could be offset in terms of swing speed. So you have a larger, lighter, stronger, and more forgiving clubhead, which has turned the golf equipment business on its head. People routinely spend up to $500 on a new driver with all that exotic material and new technology— things like weight screws that change the swing dynamics of the club, or composite crowns to get more weight down on the bottom of the head so the ball flies higher.

What the average player doesn't realize, though, is that the clubhead is much less of a factor in hitting it great than the shaft is. The shaft really is the engine that drives a club. The top shaft companies all have engineers who worked for NASA or military contractors, developing super-strong and super-light graphite for use in space or on fighter planes. These guys came over to the shaft companies so they could use that technology for the consumer market—golf shafts, fishing rods, skis, items like that. The things they can do with shafts now are just incredible—but you've also got much more variation in what you can get these days, which is definitely a challenge. I looked at Golfsmith.com, a club component Web site, the other day, and if you're looking for a graphite driver shaft in extra-stiff flex, they've got 44 different kinds. In standard flex, there are 162 choices.

One long driver—just a huge guy—routinely hits it longer than almost anybody out there. We were all watching once when he drilled one off the 370 sign so loudly that you could hear it back at the tee. But he uses shafts that are too flexible, and he can't consistently keep it on the grid. In long drive—and in regular golf—it isn't just about hitting it the farthest. You have to be accurate, too. The way a shaft loads, kicks, and torques is the difference between a mediocre tee shot and one that bombs out there. And all of those factors can be tweaked to the smallest degree.

You also can't count on shafts with the same label on them to perform the same, even if they're same model. I'll get thirty or forty shafts from the shaft company, and even though they were all made on the same run, from the same batch of graphite, no two of them are alike. You're at the mercy of the quality of the material used when the filament sheets were originally made, and how they were wound when the shafts were built. The guys who make my JLG Ultra Boom shafts are great, but there's some art—and variation—that goes with the science.

The first thing I do when I get a bundle of shafts is check them for frequency and weight. A shaft's frequency is basically how often it wiggles back and forth over a certain spot when you pull it back and let it snap back into place. The slower the club wiggles, the "softer," or more flexible, it is. I like my shafts to have 250 frequency, but they come from the plant ranging from 230 to 270—even though they're from the same batch. The last two world championships I won, the frequency of my shafts were 250 and 251, so I guess I know what I like. The shafts I get weigh between 70 and 85 grams—which is on the heavy side compared to the ultra-light shafts in a lot of standard drivers now. You can buy shafts that are 50 grams, but I think what you gain in speed (from swinging a lighter shaft) you lose because there's not as much mass behind the ball when you hit it.

Shafts are made by wrapping sheets of graphite filament around a metal die. The denser the sheets used, the stiffer the shaft is. And depending on how the sheets are placed, you can build a shaft that will bend more near the tip (tip flexible) or higher up near the grip (tip stiff). You can also adjust how much the clubhead will torque, or twist. To me, a shaft's torque is just as important as its flex. If

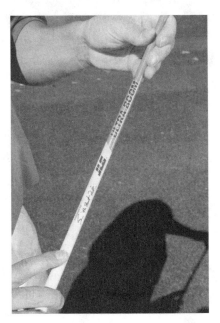

The sheets of graphite that are used to make a shaft create a seam that runs along one side. That seam is the stiffest part of the shaft, and I want it pointing straight up. My shaft company prints a logo on it so I know how to set the shaft in the clubhead.

it torques too much, the face will twist through impact and you'll hit it crooked. If it doesn't torque enough, you won't get any snap through impact, and you'll hit it shorter.

Out of a group of 40 shafts, I might find about 10 really good ones. I mark those and then treat them as if they were made of gold. Every shaft has a spine, where the seams of the filament sheets line up. That's the stiffest part of the shaft, so I orient that spine straight up, so that I'm looking down at it at address (this helps me by finding the spine and putting the JLG logo straight down it, too). That way, the spine won't prevent the shaft from loading or unloading.

Without a doubt, a good shaft is more valuable than a good head. I've had plenty of good heads (ones that looked good, were made well, and had a lively face) that I've had to switch onto a new shaft when the original shaft broke, and if the new shaft wasn't good—or even just as well suited to the clubhead as the old shaft had been—the head was pretty much a doorknob. I get my clubheads in boxes of fifty, four boxes a year. They're specially made 440 cc Dunlop heads with my name on them, built with four degrees of loft, three degrees upright, three degrees closed, and with extra material behind the face. A standard clubhead has a face 2.6 millimeters thick. Mine are 3.0, and that's the difference between caving the face in on the first or second shot, like I would with your driver, or being able to use a competition head twenty-five or thirty times before it breaks. Every once in a while, I'll get a head that goes well past thirty balls, and when that happens, the head is usually good for a hundred or more hits. Sometimes you just get an extra-strong head. That goes to show you how much variation there is the material, even with teams of technicians doing strict quality control on my special-order heads.

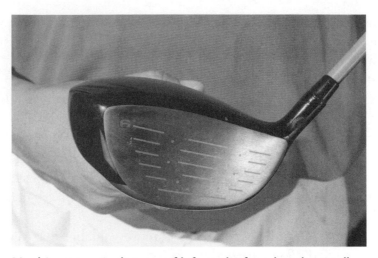

My drivers say six degrees of loft on the face, but they really have about four. They're also built with more material behind the face, so they don't cave in like a standard driver would.

I play with the same group of guys every week at Chenal (the DGA, or Doug's Golf Association—and they give me just as much crap as anybody else, which I love) here in Little Rock, and my buddies have only ever asked me to try out their drivers once. I busted the face almost in half on my friend's brand-new $300 club. I go through at least two hundred competition clubheads a year. Most of the time, the seams where the face is welded onto the body of the club start to give way. Sometimes, the whole top of the head just collapses. When you're swinging it at 150 miles per hour, it's like a car crash when the club hits the ball. If there's any little flaw in the titanium alloy material that gets pressed into one of my clubheads, I'm going to find it out pretty quickly. When a head collapses, it looks like an orange that somebody dropped off the

Just in case you needed proof that there's a lot of force
at impact when I hit a tee shot, here it is. I can usually get
twenty-five or thirty swings in competition out of a clubhead
before the face caves in or, in this case, the crown shatters.

roof of a five-story building. You can kind of tell what shape it used
to be, but it's all busted up. The picture here is of a head I broke in
2005 on my way to winning the title. Another time, I hit one and
the clubhead basically disintegrated. A shard of metal flew up and
cut me pretty badly under my right eye. I'm already legally blind in
my left eye from macular degeneration, so if that shard had gone
into my right eye, I'd have had a problem.

Throughout the year, I'm trying to find twenty or thirty solid
clubhead-shaft combinations to put in my stash for the World
Championship. When I get one that's really great, I'll write down
all the specs on the clubhead with a marker and scratch a number
onto the shaft. I keep a list with the shaft information by number,
so I can put a new head on the good shaft if the head breaks. When

I get to Mesquite for the World Championship, I feel like I have my best collection of clubs, and I'm ready to win. So much preparation has gone into those clubs that I'm always shocked to see guys second-guessing themselves in the practice time before the early rounds, switching out shafts and trying new clubheads.

Sometimes, though, even the best plans don't work exactly right. At the 2005 World Championship, I took nineteen heads with me, and after I broke seven of them the first two days, I knew I was going to run out. My wife wasn't coming out until the weekend, so I called her in Little Rock and asked her to send me the rest of the box. It's not like you can just call Taiwan and order more for next-day delivery. I broke the ones she sent, too, and I had to call her just before she flew, to grab two more heads I had left on the

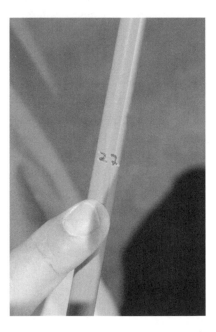

I scratch numbers into every "gamer" shaft I find, so I can cross-reference them with the little book I carry that has the specs in it. I used this shaft in the 2006 championship.

workbench because they didn't sound right. I put them on some good shafts, and those last two heads were the ones I won the 2005 championship with.

Let's be realistic here, though. The setup I use for my drivers isn't going to work for you (or for anybody else in the world, except maybe four or five other long drivers). When my clubs are put together, they have 48-inch-long shafts (compared to 45 inches for a standard club), and they're so stiff that the average guy couldn't even get it airborne. You're probably thinking, "What does this mean for me? How does it apply to the clubs in my bag?"

My 48-inch driver might not be the right choice for you, but the way I find the perfect clubhead-shaft combination *will* work for a golfer at any level—and with any clubhead speed. First, you need to completely change how you shop for a driver.

See if this sounds familiar: You're out with some buddies playing golf, and at the range before, you notice that one guy has a new driver. Doesn't matter what brand. Call it the hottest thing on tour. Whatever. Of course, you've got to try it to see if he's got something that will work for you. You swing it three or four times and just kill it out there. Your own driver seems like a six-year-old car with two more years left on the lease compared to the shiny new one. So what do you do? You go down to the nearest golf shop, put down your credit card, and buy one, probably with the same shaft your buddy's club had.

I don't care what a clubhead looks like. You might get some warm fuzzies from looking at it in the beginning, but looks don't matter. There are guys in long drive who get caught up in the latest wild shaft color or clubhead. What matters is how it's set up for you. This isn't going to be real popular with the club companies, but it's still true. Instead of writing down all the information that's printed on your buddy's clubhead, you should go get it weighed and have the shaft measured for stiffness, torque, and weight. Then go get your driver built to those specs. Because, honestly, whatever clubhead you pick, you're going to like the feel and how you hit it if it matches those particular specs, not because it's a certain brand of head.

If you walk into a store and buy a driver off the rack, it'll just be luck if it works good for you. And even if it does work, there's no doubt in my mind that you could do better by starting out hitting a bunch of drivers, then working backward from the head-shaft combinations that feel good for you.

Start by finding a good club fitter, one who uses a launch monitor. If you're a member at a private club, you probably have access to a fitter and a monitor there. If not, you can find them at most large off-course golf shops. I don't know how else to say this, so I'll just say it: if you're serious about your game, you'd be stupid not to get fitted. And it's usually free, or the cost is taken off the price of the club if you end up buying it. Seriously, there's no reason, aside from laziness, not to get fitted.

The best thing you can do when you go get fitted is make your regular swing—don't swing from the heels or try to bunt it out there—and be honest about your game. That's how you're going to get the most help from the fitter. Here are some other tips to take with you so you can walk out with the best club possible.

1. Don't walk in and buy a driver with an off-the-rack, mass-produced shaft. Equipment manufacturers put shafts in their clubs for two reasons. First, it's about cost. The shafts in those clubs can be pretty good, but mostly they're the best shaft at a certain price point. The other reason is that the menu of shafts in that style from that company is wide enough to account for the widest part of the club market. The company wants to be able to put a few different shafts in the club and satisfy most of the market without having to carry a bunch of different shafts in inventory. A driver with an off-the-rack shaft *can* be a good choice, but that's only going to be by luck. Try it, but try a bunch of other shaft-club combinations as well.

2. Buy the optimum clubhead-shaft combination. Work with a fitter who has that same goal in mind. If the guy has banners from one shaft company all over his shop and only gives you two or three choices from that company, pick a different fitter. The same is true for clubheads. Do you really think that the only possible combinations that would work for you come from Callaway or Titleist or any other single company?

3. Resist the temptation to watch a tour player and decide to go out and buy the same flex and loft setup he has. That's just as true when it comes to your buddies. Again, we're trying to find the best driver for *you*.

4. No two shafts are the same. That holds true both for individual examples of the same model of shaft and for shafts across different companies. Two JLG Ultra Boom stiff shafts with a low kick point aren't the same, just like Harrison's "stiff" shaft is different from Aldila's, which is different from AccuFLEX's.

5. Forget your preconceived notions about shaft flex. What is flex? It's how much (or how little) the shaft bends when you swing it. In a perfect setup, a shaft loads when you make your backswing and unloads (unbends) predictably down through impact, giving you more speed. If you use a shaft that's too stiff, the club never loads or unloads completely. You're going to hit the ball low and right. If you use a shaft that's too flexible, the club loads too much, then unloads unpredictably through impact. If I use a regular-flex shaft, it's like I'm trying to hit a shot with a clubhead that's attached to a strand of overcooked spaghetti. The shaft makes the clubhead flop around, and I don't feel like I'm in control.

People ask me all the time what flex shaft they should use. It doesn't matter what I think, or even what it says on the shaft itself. What matters is that the stiffness of the shaft you use matches your swing. That might mean a regular-flex Aldila shaft or a light Fujikura shaft, depending on the particular company and model. It's not just about how far you hit it, or how far you carry the ball. Most players I play with wildly overestimate how far they hit it, and most of them use shafts that are way too stiff. Unless you're legitimately carrying the ball 225 yards (and that's probably no more than 15 percent of the golf population), you shouldn't be worrying too much about whether or not your shaft is too flexible for you.

6. Torque is way, way more important than kick point. A lot of new shafts are being advertised as "low kick point" or "high kick point," and "tip stiff" or "tip soft." Where a shaft bends, or kicks, most along its length is a factor in how the shaft performs, but it is a much bigger deal when you swing 150 miles per hour than when you swing 100 miles per hour. I need to have my shafts built with more material near the grip end and near the tip, because otherwise I'll break it at the top of my backswing near the grip or through impact when the clubhead releases. You don't have those same problems. How much a shaft torques is a much bigger deal for every play—amateurs included.

7. Loft is just one element of launch angle—the angle at which the ball leaves the clubface after impact. A lot of players get caught up in what loft driver they use. Now, having the right loft is important, but you need to have the right loft working together with your other shaft specifications. My driver has four degrees of loft on it. When an average player picks up my club and sees that, he wonders how anybody could hit anything more than a low line drive. But with that four-degree driver, my launch angle is still 14 degrees—the same as a tour player's. I need a low-loft driver for the tremendous snap and release I have at impact. If I used a 10-degree club, I'd hit the ball way, way too high, with way too much spin, and lose distance.

The average guy has the opposite problem. Most players use a shaft that's too stiff and a club that doesn't have enough loft. Combined, those things are deadly in terms of reaching the optimum launch angle. The stiff shaft already makes it hard to get height on the ball if you don't have enough speed, and using a 9- or 10-degree face just adds to the problem. Your goal when you get fit for a driver is to put together a shaft-clubhead combo that gets you into that 14- or 15-degree launch angle sweet spot. That gives you the best combination of carry and roll.

Just remember that adding loft only works to a point. Some average players have been going with 13- or even 14-degree drivers in an effort to get their launch angle up. But the more loft you use, the more of a glancing blow you put on a ball, and the more backspin you add. At the World Championship in 2005, a lot of players were going to seven- and eight-degree drivers, but I stuck with my four-degree, because I didn't want to have more of that glancing blow on the back of the ball. Most players would do great with a 10- or 11-degree club with the right shaft specs.

Your longest drives come from the right combination of loft angle and backspin. When you get on the launch monitor, what you'll probably discover is that you need to hit the ball higher and with more backspin than you expected to get your maximum carry. In long driving, it's easy to say what that "sweet spot" combination is, because we all swing at pretty much the same speed. If it's a calm day and we're hitting in medium conditions at sea level, a 12.5-degree launch angle with 2,200 rpms of backspin is ideal. If the ground gets soft, I might want my launch angle to get up to 15 degrees and my spin down to 1,800 rpms—things you can change with both your swing and the club you use. The sweet spot for you is going to depend on your particular swing—which is why you need to get fitted.

8. Don't overlook weight, both in the clubhead and the shaft. When I was playing softball, the newest bats got lighter and lighter, until a lot of players were using 28-ounce bats. But the technology got to the point where the bats were so light that you could swing really fast but there wasn't enough mass behind the strike to make the ball go far. My advice is to use the heaviest shaft-clubhead combination you can swing at your top swing speed. Anything lighter than that is just a waste, especially since ultra-light shafts are way more expensive than "standard" ones. For most players, that's going to mean a shaft of about 70 grams for a 45-inch club. Speed is important in a swing, but mass is important, too.

I've heard about some long drivers back-weighting their club with some weight inside the grip, the theory being that the swing weight will be changed by the counterweight, making the club will feel lighter. I've experimented with it, and the clubhead does *feel* lighter, but it didn't translate into more actual clubhead speed. I actually take weight off the grip end of my drivers by using very thin grips—about half the thickness of standard ones. The thinner grips help me move my hands quicker.

9. Go by feel, not by brand. One of the things a lot of people don't realize is that the same foundries make most of the clubheads you buy. The technology and designs are a little different, but the foundries are the same, and the same guys in China and Taiwan are building them. The fact is, people are so caught up in brand names and smoke-and-mirrors marketing that they don't make decisions based on the most important thing—how the club feels to hit. In the extreme world of long driving, two of the recent World Championships have been won with a club that's been associated with Wal-Mart and Kmart. I had a $150 Dunlop clubhead, going up against guys using $500 clubheads. My new Sean Fister signature model is going to be a little more expensive, but not as much as the premium brands. The premium companies make good stuff, but just remember that expensive doesn't necessarily mean better.

10. Keep up with technology. Not all the stuff coming from club companies is hype. There have been some real advances in weighting and aerodynamics, and drivers are getting more forgiving every year. You can make a less-than-perfect swing and still get pretty good results. You don't need to buy a new driver every season, but if your driver is more than two years old, you're giving up distance and/or consistency to your playing partners. I'm not saying you should dump a driver you love and hit great. Instead, get its weight and frequency measured, then get a new model built to those same specs. You can keep hitting the older one as long as you like, but I bet that if you try the new one, built to the right specs, you'll be pleasantly surprised.

Picking the wrong golf ball to go with your new driver can waste all the work that went into your club fitting. Remember how we said that a 14-degree launch angle is ideal, regardless of how hard you swing? When you're getting fitted for a driver, you're trying to generate between 2,500 and 3,000 rpms in backspin on your shot. If you generate more, the ball is going to balloon up in the air or curve off line. If you generate less, you won't get the lift backspin creates with the dimples on the ball.

What does that mean for you? Well, it depends. I generate a lot of clubhead speed, and I'm looking for less ball spin, not more. Harder balls will go longer because they don't spin too much and they don't deform as much off the driver when you hit them.

But what happens if you don't generate enough backspin? If you have less swing speed, say 80 miles per hour (which means you carry your drive about 180 yards), you need to launch the ball higher, with a club that has more loft. You also need a ball that's going to help you get more spin. If you can get your spin up to 3,000 rpms or even a little more, the properties of the ball (the dimples and the way they are organized) are going to give you more carry distance.

One thing I can tell you is that unless you generate a good amount of clubhead speed, like 110 miles per hour (again, the average player swings about 90), you shouldn't waste your money on the top-of-the-line, multicover tour balls. First, if you don't swing fast enough to compress the layers of the ball together at impact with your driver, you don't get the benefit of the technology. Also, if you're not shooting scores in the 70s, your swing isn't consistent enough for you to be able to see the difference in your performance in terms of the ball. You're also not swinging fast enough to generate a lot of backspin with your short irons, so not having a ball that spins a lot with the wedges isn't going to make much difference.

There are many good balls out there in the $15 to $20 per dozen range, and they can do 90 percent of what the most expensive tour balls can do. You want to pick the one that gives you the best launch condition off your driver, and the best feel when you hit chips and putts. If a ball feels too "hard" when you chip or putt, even if it doesn't actually perform any differently than a "softer" ball, you aren't going to putt and chip as well with it. Dunlop (and other companies) are now making "distance" balls with a variety of different cover compositions. The balls perform the same way in terms of distance and spin, but they have different feels off the shorter clubs.

To finish up, I'll tell you a little about the rest of my set. When I play a regular round of golf, I use basically the same driver I'd use in a competition—maybe not the exact same club I'm going to take to Mesquite, but one with the same specs. I want to get as much experience hitting to defined targets (like fairways) as I can, with the same kind of club I'm going to use to hit on the grid. After the driver, I have a one-iron for when I've got a tight fairway, and then a four-iron down through pitching wedge. After that, I've got three other wedges that range from 52 to 66 degrees. I hit the one-iron 320, the four-iron 240, and my pitching wedge 175. All my clubs are Dunlop tour models.

I'll tell you one thing—nothing burns me more than standing over a tee shot to a tight fairway and making a baby swing with my one-iron to try to hit one straight and pushing it into the woods. Standing there 240 yards from the green, in the trees, I'm always kicking myself for not hitting driver. If you're going to be in the trees, you might as well be as close as you can to the green.

In other words, get a driver you like and go for it. Laying up is for wimps.

8

DRILLS AND TIPS

There are two pieces to getting the power swing I've been talking about in this book. The first piece is to get setup mechanics down. If you can get yourself in a good, athletic position before you start, you're going to make it so much easier on yourself when it comes time to swing. We covered those details in chapters 3 and 4—grip, stance, posture, foot position, and spine tilt.

The second piece is where all the magic happens, so to speak. Once you have a good setup and you understand the basics of what you want to do with your swing, the next step is feel. It's getting a sense of what the power move feels like. It sounds funny, but most players don't know what it feels like to generate real speed with a golf club. They've spent so much time trying to manipulate the club into position that they've never created a free-swinging move where the clubhead just rips through the air.

Let's talk about some drills and swing images that are going to make that feel happen for you. I've played a lot of sports in my life—I pole-vaulted, played softball, and threw the discus and the javelin, just to name a few. What I found is that hitting a golf ball involves the same kind of power positions and dynamic moves that other ball sports or throwing sports do.

In other words, hitting a golf ball is a lot closer to things you probably already know how to do, at least in terms of pivoting or shifting your weight. Even if you've never played any other sport, I'm sure you can take a hammer and pound in a nail without thinking much about it. When you hit the nail, you don't stick your elbow out or try to throw the head of the hammer out at the top of your swing. You use your wrist at the end of the swing, to bring the hammer down on the nail with some power. That move is the same one you use when you hit a golf ball.

To get a feel for keeping your head back and slinging your hands through impact, take a ball and throw it sidearm down the fairway, as if you were skipping a rock.

When I give a corporate clinic, I always call a few guys up to hit some balls and give them a few pointers. When I'm trying to get across the idea of speed, I start with a simple demonstration. I'm sure you've skipped rocks across a lake before. What kid hasn't? To skip a rock, you know you have sling it sidearm, with lots of wrist action, to get the flat part of the rock skipping across the water. I take a ball and sling it down the fairway just like I would a rock. My head stays back. I make a natural pivot to throw. Then I toss a ball to the guy who's up for the demonstration, and he does the same thing easily. In fact, I can count on one hand the number of guys I've done that experiment with who didn't immediately get that slinging-rock feeling and how it applies to hitting a golf ball.

Another image that works great for golf is swinging a bat with power. Think about it: have you ever swung a bat and flipped your wrists at the ball when the bat was still behind your head? I doubt it. Something seems to change when we bend over and address a ball with a golf club instead of swinging at one that's flying toward us. I think it has to do with the amount of time there is to think in golf compared to the time you have in baseball. In baseball or softball, you react to the ball as it comes to you. In golf, you have to apply the force to the ball to make it go. But the mechanics of a good baseball or softball swing are similar to a golf swing. I actually like to take a bat and swing it at a heavy bag hanging in my basement, because the muscles I'm building with that swing are the same as the ones in my golf swing.

The "snap" power hitters have at impact is another feel that some players have trouble visualizing. If you've ever played racquetball, you already know what snap feels like. If you swing a racquetball racquet with just your body or just your arm, the ball won't go very fast at all. Your buddy will track it down easily and wear you out. To make the ball jump off the racquet, you've got

Notice how my weight transfers forward to swing the bat through impact . . .

. . . but my upper body doesn't push forward at all. My head stays back, and I'm pivoting against my straight left leg. The speed of the swing . . .

to give it some zip at impact by juicing it with some wrist action. In fact, that wrist action is the reason a lot of tennis players—who don't use much wrist action in those strokes—get smoked when they first try to play racquetball.

To get a sense for what that snap feels like, stand in your golf stance and hold a racquetball racket in your right hand. Ask a friend to toss you a Ping-Pong ball, and try to whack that ball as hard as you can. You won't even need anybody to tell you how to

. . . is what pulls me forward at the end.

get the speed up. It's intuitive. Now start using some of that speed at impact with your golf swing.

You can also use a variety of different training aids to help get your swing where it needs to be more quickly than if you just swing a club. I started using a weighted club called the Momentus years ago, and the same company that makes it came out with a new weighted club called the Power Hitter that you can actually hit balls with. It's great for working on balance, because you can't pull that heavy weight off plane without falling over. Hit twenty-five balls with the Power Hitter, then switch back and hit twenty-five with your normal club, then repeat that sequence. You'll ingrain a

The head of the racquet trails my arm right up to impact, and then I snap my wrist to add a lot more speed.

balanced, on-plane move, and swinging the weighted club will also work as a dynamic weightlifting session—but with your real golf move.

The Swing Fan is another cool tool I use at least five times a week. It's a shortened golf shaft with four big fan blades on the end. The blades cause wind resistance when you swing, and more of it the faster you swing. The way to develop fast-twitch muscle fibers is to confuse your muscles with heavy weights and then light ones. The muscles then adapt to be ready for either kind of load. The Swing Fan recruits all those fibers. I swing it twenty or thirty times a morning, five days a week.

When I really want to get medieval, I pull out the SpeedChain—which really does look like something out of the Middle Ages. It's a golf shaft with a 20- or 30-foot-long chain of heavy links attached to the bottom. You get on the grass and sling the chain back and forth as if you were cracking a whip. It's a brutal exercise, and five minutes of it once a week is enough to really develop strength and speed in your core muscles.

The last trainer I use is the XLR8R—a golf shaft with a ball attached to the end of it. The ball has Velcro strips on it, and when you swing across a special platform the strips stick on it if you're making solid, square contact. If the face comes through open or closed, the ball just bounces off the platform. It obviously encourages you to hit the ball solid, but anticipating the ball sticking on the platform also really teaches you to accelerate the club at impact. It's a great tool.

The other drills and practice techniques I use are all directly related to withstanding the mental and physical pressure that comes when I get to the World Championship. I already told you about playing move the towel—hitting sequences of six balls against a friend, with the guy who hits the longest ball out of the six getting to "own" the towel. That's a great game, and a lot of fun to play against a buddy for a little cash on the line. It really motivates you when you lose the towel, and you work hard to try to win it back.

I also like to do sets of swing drills in the weight room, with weights instead of a golf club. Making technically sound swings with extra load on your muscles does a couple of things. It helps you build strength, obviously, but it also forces you to make the motion more slowly, which ingrains it more quickly.

The lat pull-down machine is great for this kind of drill. I connect the V-bar (a V-shaped handle with a ring at the point of the

V) and stand so my feet are quartering away from the machine. I start from my top-of-backswing position and pull the entire stack on the machine down to the impact position. This exercise works directly on the shoulder girdle, the muscle responsible for generating power. I can do three sets of 10 with the whole stack of weights (250 pounds), but you might want to start with 40 or 50 pounds and work your way up.

The Kill Grid

One element of my serious practice for the World Championship is great for any player to incorporate into his routine. I call it the Kill Grid. Every practice session, I keep track of each shot I hit, in six-ball rounds. I've actually got spreadsheets set up on my computer that I print out, and I mark them with the date and keep them in a notebook year by year.

I go out to the ninth hole at my club and I complete at least 20 rounds—20 six-ball sessions—during each practice day. I record how many shots I hit solid, or "killed," and the number I hit in the fairway. So for each round, I have a total number of kills, a total number of balls in the grid, and kill and grid percentages.

The fairway on that hole is 38 yards wide, which is narrower than the grid at the championship. By charting all my drives and their dispersion, I get a much better feel for my swing and equipment. When it comes to dialing in your equipment, real-life conditions are always more helpful than what you can get from the information on a launch monitor. I'm not saying the monitors aren't helpful. They are. But the problem is that most people get on them and get caught up in the speed numbers—myself included—and they want to see how fast they can swing, or how high they can get the ball speed reading. That might be fun, but it can wreck your golf swing. You want to be careful how you use the monitor to check your launch condition. Break your time on it into three 20-ball sessions but don't ask for the results until the end of each session. That way, you aren't going for the instant gratification of a big monitor number. Then blend the results of all three sessions together when you're determining what specs you need.

When I'm filling out my Kill Grid every day, my goal is to have a grid percentage of 50 percent at minimum for every practice session and a kill percentage of 30 percent, minimum. Keeping my stats like this really gives me focus for each of my practice sessions, and it gives my practice sessions some of the same feel as a championship round.

Tips from the Long-Drive Bible

In this book, I've gone into a lot of detail and explanation about the things that have come out of my Long-Drive Bible, and how I came up with those tips. I thought it would be interesting to show you exactly what some of the pages in the little black book that I carry in my bag look like.

The book actually looks like a little photo album, with plastic sleeves where I can slide in pieces of paper. The first part of the Bible has my swing keys for a given year—ones that apply to how I'm hitting the ball at that time. Some years I have more trouble with losing shots to the right, so there will be more antislice tips and swing thoughts on my list. Other years I want to hit the ball higher, so those tips are more common. After that, I have a comprehensive list of the tips and swing thoughts we've been talking about here—the guts of the Bible, so to speak.

At the end of the book, I have some blank pages that I can actually pull out at a practice session or at the championship and write down new tips or swing thoughts that really seem to work. I like having a book that I can carry in my bag easily. It's a great record of what I've been working on, and I refer to it all the time to remind myself what things worked the last time I had the same kind of problem.

I go down the list of tips and try them one by one until I come up with the one that solves my problem. For me, my crooked shots usually come because I'm moving laterally off the ball on my backswing. Then my timing is off, so I shift my weight hard to the left the downswing and lunge at it. I'm going for rotation, which is far better than trying to time a weight shift or slide.

Since I dug all the tips out of the ground myself and have twenty years of experience using them, it doesn't take long to work my way down the menu to find the one I need. You're going to find that's the case for you, the more you use the tips I've been talking about.

Following are some of the key points I included in my book in 2005. Keep in mind that a few of the ideas you're going to read might be counter to what I've been talking about in the book. That's because I might be overcooking something, like firing my hips, and I need something to counter it and get back to "neutral." Still, you won't go wrong trying any of these in your quest for more power.

2005 Swing Keys

1. Hood face.

2. Light grip.

3. Slow takeaway.

4. Solid contact.

5. Quiet hips.

6. Clubhead through toward intended path.

7. Eighty-five percent effort, solid contact (swing club, not hit at it).

8. Arms extended for long takeaway.

9. Shoulder set for intended trajectory.

10. Deep breath to relax before shot.

11. Be confident.

12. Be calm and relaxed; relaxed muscles move faster.

Address

1. Feet slightly wider than shoulders.

2. Right knee flexed toward left heel.

3. Spine tilted away from target.

4. Shoulders slightly closed.

5. Left shoulder even with ball.

6. Head six inches behind ball and turned 20 degrees to the right.

7. Right foot pointed straight ahead.

8. Hands should be at impact position at address.

9. Should feel extension of arms at address.

10. Ball position forward and tee higher for upswing contact.

11. Stand tall at address.

12. At address, think only of target.

13. Hip tilted with right lower than left.

14. Wider platform for shallower path to ball.

15. Start with hands slightly behind ball.

16. Strong right-hand grip for lower ball flight.

17. Stand at a comfortable distance from ball, not too far away.

18. Right elbow tucked toward right hip.

19. Light grip pressure for more clubhead speed.

20. Left thumb on right side of shaft.

21. Close gap between thumb and forefingers on both hands.

22. Right forearm should be closer to ball than left.

23. Squat for power.

24. Sometimes, tight grip helps control.

Takeaway

1. Slow and low.

2. Left arm should move in line with clubhead to hip height.

3. Turn left shoulder to replace right shoulder position.

4. Left shoulder should go under and past chin.

5. Minimize lifting of left heel but don't have to eliminate it.

6. Minimize rotation of left knee, but can move laterally to right some.

7. Limit wrist rolling on takeaway.

8. Slow, deliberate takeaway promotes good tempo and solid contact.

9. Bigger shoulder turn and longer backswing creates more club speed.

10. Rotate, don't slide. Limit hip rotation in takeaway.

11. Right knee should not move until after impact

12. Delay wrist cock on takeaway.

13. Take club straight back along intended flight path. Grip end should point at target.

14. Keep hands as far away from chest as possible. Think long arms.

15. Create as much gap as possible between left shoulder and left hip to store power.

16. Do not allow clubhead to get inside swing plane on backswing.

17. At waist high in backswing, right arm should be higher than left arm.

18. Checkpoint for takeaway is to point grip end at target.

19. Do not drop left shoulder on takeaway. Should turn level.

20. Weight shift to right should be with upper body, not hips, turning left shoulder over right knee. Remember not to rotate either knee.

21. Keep clubhead square during takeaway, don't roll wrists.

22. Back of left hand should be straight with no bend at waist height in backswing.

23. Head can move laterally back on takeaway, but not forward on downswing.

24. Keep head behind ball until after impact.

25. Turn back toward target in backswing.

26. Stay over ball during backswing.

27. Turning left toe in can help square clubhead.

28. Smooth transition delays release (helps over the top).

Downswing

1. Initiate downswing with lower body, firing a rotation of hips, not a slide. Hips should lead arms and then hands while maintaining balance point behind ball position, while laterally shifting lower body weight onto left side, keeping left leg straight and posted against lateral sliding.

2. Shoulders should take same path down as backswing.

3. Should feel hands being dragged behind arms and shoulders in downswing.

4. Keep hands ahead of clubhead in downswing for increased arm-to-shaft angle for speed.

5. Right shoulder should pass under chin not around. Causes flare-out and resulting slice.

6. Keep left shoulder behind ball at impact.

7. Lead clubhead with right knee on downswing; remember to stay behind ball.

8. Swing clubhead through impact zone and release to target.

9. During downswing, focus on attacking ball from inside path to target, but remain behind ball.

10. Hold angle between left arm and shaft as long as possible (wrist cock), releasing snap while in balance with head behind ball.

11. Right forearm should be under left forearm approaching target.

12. At impact, right knee should not be closer to ball than left knee.

13. The faster the left shoulder unwinds, the faster the clubhead speed.

14. Keep head behind ball at impact.

15. Left wrist should be flat at impact.

One of the side benefits from working so much on my power swing is that my real-life golf game has gotten pretty good. I've got a plus-2 handicap at my home course, which is pretty wide open, but I'm a legitimate 2 or 3 handicap anywhere I play. I see myself as a regular golfer when I'm not doing my day job, and just like any regular guy, I don't have time to work on my game as much as I'd like to. If I have time to play, I'm doing it with my buddies in the DGA, to blow off steam.

I don't kid myself about being able to play with the big boys on the PGA Tour. I do one thing really well. Those guys are the decathletes of golf. They can all hit it long, hit it straight, and chip and putt. I know my place, and it's in the tee box swinging as hard as I can. I'll go out to Chenal's short game area and work on my chipping and putting a little bit, to keep my game sharp for pro-am rounds. Actually, most of my non-long-driving work comes from between 50 and 80 yards from the green, because that's where I am after my tee shot on most par-4s.

Like I said in the second chapter, I'm a self-taught player. I get a lot of questions from pro-am partners about golf instruction, and what the average guy should look for in a teacher—and if he should even get lessons. In my opinion, everybody should have a person they can go to for some critical advice on how to swing better, play better, think better, pick the right equipment, or all of the above. That can certainly be the PGA teacher at your club, but it doesn't necessarily have to be. It might be a really good player at your club whose opinion you trust.

One thing I will say about PGA teachers is that, for the most part, they've had plenty of training in how to work with a variety of different players. I'm not trying to put your particular pro down, but don't necessarily take lessons from the home pro just because he's there and convenient. You want to work with somebody who understands your swing and personality—and you want to be learning from somebody who has the same attitude about the game as you do. If you want to have fun, and in the process get a little better, you need a teacher with a lighter touch. If you want to grind it out, with a minimum of small talk, you need to find somebody more no-nonsense. Don't forget that you're going to be spending a lot of money on lessons. Making a good choice up front will save you money and aggravation.

How many lessons are enough? That's up to you to decide. You definitely need more than one, if only to get a sense of what the teacher wants you to work on and a chance to come back and test how you've progressed on those first goals. Most teachers will offer a package of three or six lessons for a discounted price off the single-lesson rate. I like those packages because they motivate you to keep at it rather than just looking for a quick fix.

I want to say one last thing before I let you go, and it fits with what we're talking about here—drills and working hard to improve your game. I'm no different from most people my age or a bit older. I notice that words like "respect" or "pay your dues" seem almost antique, or "old school." I guess that makes me old school, because I believe that the shortest and easiest route to greatness is to buckle down and work hard. If it's in you, how will you ever find out if you don't dig it out yourself? When you go out and earn your lot in life, something happens to you, and it's called self-esteem.

I'm living proof that if you work hard and try hard, you can achieve almost anything. That sounds kind of corny, I know, but it's true. I hope the tips I've shared here will help you with your game, but even if they haven't, I hope I at least left you with the idea that the hand you're dealt in life doesn't have to determine how you end up, if you're willing to make things happen for yourself.

Good luck, and give it all you've got.

9

THE FUTURE OF LONG DRIVING

There isn't any doubt that the World Long-Drive Championship is the centerpiece of our sport. It's the only event most people ever see, when it's broadcast on ESPN over the Christmas holiday. Now, I don't want to sound like I'm ungrateful for the money and attention I've gotten—both directly from the championship in purses and because of the prestige that comes with winning it. In a lot of ways, this sport has been very good to me. But I think it's stalling, and I'd like to see that change.

The reality is that we're getting less attention now than in 2001, when my win at the championship was broadcast over and over as an ESPN Classic. Part of the reason for this is that the sports broadcasting world has gotten a lot more crowded, with things like the X Games and even Ultimate Fighting, which is doing huge business in pay-per-view. There are so many more channels on even the basic cable package, like ESPN2, the Fox Sports regional channels, and even the Golf Channel, but that just gives the sports fan even more choices about what to watch (and what to switch away from).

I think the main problem we have in the sport of long driving is that we're not doing enough to create stars and promote the personalities we have. We're not making our big event a "must-watch." And I say this as one of the two most famous guys in the sport. I'm not talking so much about how I should be getting more publicity, but about coming up with a better way to showcase the personalities and rivalries that make any sport exciting. I think fans are always going to be impressed by guys who can hit the ball 400 yards, but I look at what NASCAR does with its marketing and promotion and think that we should be paying more attention to that kind of model. It's about guys who drive 200 miles per hour, but it's also about what Dale Earnhardt Jr. is doing versus what Tony Stewart and Jeff Gordon are doing. The personalities and rivalries are a fundamental part of the equation—not just the speed and the cars.

How do we do that in long driving? Two ways: by creating an independent league and by reformatting the World Championship.

The way the sport is organized now, one guy—Art Sellinger—owns both the biggest event and the sport's governing body, the Long Drivers of America. I have a lot of respect for Art's business sense, and he's been very shrewd about building the World Championship into a successful business vehicle. He deserves a tremendous amount of credit for doing all the hard work of getting the championship on ESPN and making it a first-class event for the hitters. I know better than anybody else what a big deal it is to win that title.

But Art's interest is in the event being as financially successful as possible—for him. And I don't blame him one bit for that. Hey, he's a business owner. Let's not be naive here. Art has his own sponsorship interests at stake at the championship—like equipment companies he endorses and competitors he represents as an agent—that are priorities for him. He has a sponsorship deal with

Pinnacle, and Pinnacle also sponsors the World Championship. That means we all have to hit Pinnacle balls in the event, even if we're sponsored by other companies. I don't think that's fair, but I can understand it. The only point I'm trying to make is that if we're trying to identify the best hitter in the world—at an independent "world championship"—fairness needs to be taken into consideration.

What we need to grow is to be an independent league—run by the players, with a commissioner hired by the league—that has as its one main goal promoting the sport as a whole. The PGA Tour is a nonprofit organization set up to get the players the best and most profitable deals in terms of tournaments and television exposure. As a group, Tour players get rich if the sport becomes more popular, and the guys who play the best (and have the most charisma) get the richest. It follows that the centerpiece of my sport—the World Championship—should be run by an organization that represents all of the hitters equally, not some of them a little more "equally" than others.

I look at what's happening with Ultimate Fighting and I can't help but feel a little bit jealous. Here's a sport that wasn't even on the radar five years ago—in fact, it was getting banned by state after state because of how brutal it was. It's still brutal now—getting punched full in the face always is. But they made some rules to rein in some of the blood, which allowed the fights to be sanctioned by the athletic commissions in most states. More important, the people who organize the sport knew that they had some colorful personalities they could market more aggressively—just like wrestling has done for years. More than a million people paid $39.95 to watch the big Chuck Liddell–Tito Ortiz match on pay-per-view in December 2006. They didn't spend that money just to watch two unknown guys beat each other up.

Go to the Ultimate Fighting Web site and you can look up Chuck Liddell's career record, watch videos of his fights, buy merchandise with his picture on it, and find out where to see the next fight. That sport does a great job building stars and getting rivalries going, and fans respond to that. If you like Chuck Liddell—or Tim Sylvia or Randy Couture—you can get as much information as you'd ever want about them from the Web site.

When it comes to promoting long driving, I think there are two ways to do it. You could push the idea that anybody can pay his $40 at a local qualifier and take his shot at getting under the lights in Mesquite at the championship. The U.S. Open in regular golf has that element to it, with its local and sectional qualifiers.

I think the grassroots element of the sport is important—after all, it's how I came up through the ranks. The idea that anybody with the talent to do this, and a little bit of luck, could make it to the top definitely makes for a good Cinderella story.

But when it comes to television, I think stars drive the show. The people at ESPN want to see names they recognize, both from previous years' championships and from the marketing that the sport should be doing for the hitters who are at the top of the sport currently. In other words, I think it's great for the sport when *any* hitter gets famous for his ability and his charisma. It pulls along the rest of the guys in the sport, and we should be doing everything we can to promote those guys to the general public—regardless of what logos they wear on their shirts. If the sport gets more exposure and better ratings on ESPN, everybody wins. More sponsors get interested, and the amounts they're willing to spend get bigger.

When it comes to the championship itself, I believe there are ways to do a better job identifying who truly is the longest driver in the world, and also putting on a better, more exciting show for the fans.

1. Make it a bigger deal to actually get to the finals in Mesquite. I love the idea that a guy can win his way through local and sectional tournaments and get to the big show. But the big show should really be about the best in the world. I'd limit the field at the World Championship to 50, instead of the 128 that qualify now. I'd also reorganize the local and sectional qualifiers so that they operate on the exact same format as the finals. Now you can go to your local qualifier and hit until your money runs out—$40 for each set of six balls. In the sectionals, there are bye rounds for guys who won their local qualifiers. Guys who are new to the sport get to Mesquite and they don't have a chance, because they've never competed in the elimination format used there.

2. Take as much luck out of it as possible. I'd start by putting a barrier across the grid. To get into the field, you have to be able to carry the barrier when it's at 300 yards. That would separate the guys who can't hit it out of their shadow and could potentially make it through on a freak bounce off a hard spot on the ground. In the finals, the group of 50 would get in a line and hit three balls over the barrier, starting at 300 yards. You'd get three chances to hit three balls, which would even out the impact of temperature and wind. Basically, you'd be hitting three balls three times for a total of nine balls, with an hour wait in between each session. After the first round, the guys who carried the 300-yard barrier would move on, and the ones who didn't would go home. The barrier would then be moved to 310 yards, and the guys who were left would go again, and so on.

The winner would essentially be the last man standing. If there were two guys left, and the barrier was 370 yards out, each guy would have one round of nine balls to clear it. If one guy did and the other didn't, the one who did would be the champion. If both guys cleared it, you'd alternate shots. If one guy cleared it and the other guy couldn't match, game over.

3. Add some excitement to every round. I'd find a sponsor to put up $5,000 for every shot that carried a second barrier, at, say, 380 yards. That would make every ball in the tournament a potential "money ball." You could even build a grid that had water as the second barrier, with a black landing area and big lights around it. I think that'd make for a lot more drama on television, with balls splashing down in the water and the crowd screaming and groaning. Clearing a barrier would also take all the second-guessing and excuses out of the event. You wouldn't be able to knock some guy for getting a lucky bounce off a hard spot. You'd have to earn it.

And because of the smaller field size, you could promote the hell out of each guy, putting his complete record and bio on a Web site and giving fans a chance to really know who they're rooting for.

4. Build some rivalries with barnstorming tours earlier in the year. If you've read this far, you know this sport is about strength, willpower, ego, and testosterone. Why not take advantage of that? I'd send groups of five long drivers on tours in different parts of the country to have shootouts at local ranges. Leading up to each shootout, I'd publicize a king-of-the-hill match between anybody who wanted to come out and qualify—for free, to weed out anybody who's just wasting time—and take on the winner of the shootout. I'd take $5,000 in cash and set it next to the tee. If one of the locals hit the long ball, he'd get the $5,000 on the spot.

Believe me, I'm not protective of any of these ideas. I want the sport to get bigger and better, and if that starts with the LDA taking some of these ideas and running with them, fine. But I know we can do better.

I also want to say one last thing about the marketing individual guys do in relation to long driving. Because we don't have a real league to go along with the World Championship, there are a lot of guys out there who promote themselves as the longest hitter or the world record holder or the world champion. This guy Jack Hamm calls himself a six-time world champion so he can sell a driver on an infomercial. I've never seen him at the finals in Mesquite. Not once. Basically, anybody can claim some kind of record or title and use that to sign a marketing deal and entertain corporate clients. When those guys can't deliver in terms of being able to hit the ball like a real top-level long driver, the sport suffers. Guys like Zuback and Sellinger have earned the right to call themselves champions, and the benefits that come with that. We owe it to the fans and to the companies interested in using long drivers for promotional events to provide a more organized way to identify who the best are. You don't claim to be a world champion golfer if you never played on the PGA Tour (or maybe the European Tour), just like nobody calls a guy who makes his ten-mile drive to work in a really fast time the NASCAR season champion. We shouldn't let it happen in this sport either.

THE BEAST CARD

Sean "the Beast" Fister

Height: 6 foot 5

Weight: 245 pounds

Born: Chillicothe, Missouri, June 12, 1962

Home: Little Rock, Arkansas

Long Drivers of America Hall of Fame inductee, 2002

Three-time world champion (1995, 2001, 2005)

2002 international champion

Three-time captain, U.S. Long-Drive Team

Arkansas Golf Hall of Fame inductee, 2007

Longest recorded drive: 515 yards

Longest drive in competition: 450 yards

Fastest recorded clubhead speed: 171.2 mph

Fastest recorded ball speed: 218 mph

World Championship Record

1989: missed cut (MC)

1993: MC

1994: 5th

1995: champion

1996: MC

1997: 2nd

1998: 6th

1999: 7th

2000: 10th

2001: champion

2002: MC

2003: MC

2004: MC

2005: champion

2006: MC

Other Accomplishments in Long Driving

- 2006: Competed (as reigning world champion) in eight National Long-Drive Competitions in Asia, sponsored by Dunlop Sports in Asia, winning all eight with an average winning margin of 70 yards.

- 2005: Inducted into Poplar Bluff (Missouri) Sports Hall of Fame.

- 2005: Semifinal drive carried 395 yards, the longest carry in World Championship finals history.

- 2002: Captained U.S. Long-Drive Team to victory over International Team, hitting final drive 444 yards to Jason Zuback's 434, sealing the team victory.

- 2004: LDA Tour winner in Des Moines, Iowa (became oldest winner ever on LDA Tour).

- 1997: Fiber X World Class Invitational winner.

- 1997: Tournament of Champions winner, Cincinatti.

Records

- American distance record in World Championship final round, 406 yards in 1997.

- Oldest Open Division World Championship winner at age forty-three, in 2005 (and second oldest at thirty-nine in 2001).

- Longest span from first to last championship win at ten years, one month.
- Only American to win three Open Division championships.
- Highest ball speed ever recorded at Dunlop Player Test Facility at 218 mph.
- Highest clubhead speed ever recorded at Motion Reality Sports, Inc. at 171.2 mph.
- Set World Championship–winning drive distance record in 1995 at 362 yards, 12 inches, breaking the twenty-three-year-old record set by Evan "Big Cat" Williams at 352 yards.
- Held record for championship-winning margin at 12 yards (1995).
- Won eleven state and regional long-drive competitions.
- Other:
  - World-class pole vaulter, javelin thrower, and decathlete; trained under Chairman of Olympic Decathlon Development Mike Bozeman for 1988 Olympics.
  - Attended University of Florida on athletic scholarship for pole-vault, javelin, and decathlon for fourth and fifth years of collegiate eligibility. Was undefeated in regular season in pole-vault in 1985. Personal record in pole-vault is 17′ 7″.
  - Held number one rank in NAIA in pole-vault in 1983 while at Park University.
  - Held Poplar Bluff High School record in pole-vault for twenty years.
  - Holds Poplar Bluff Morrow Stadium record in pole-vault at 17′ (set in 1986).

- Holds Park University pole-vault record at 15′ 10″ (set in 1980).

The Five Best Long Drivers of All Time (for Now)

1. Jason Zuback—1996, 1997, 1998, 1999, 2006 world champion

2. Sean "The Beast" Fister—1995, 2001, 2005 world champion

3. Evan "Big Cat" Williams—1976, 1977 national champion

4. Fred Hooter—three world titles in senior and super senior divisions

5. Mike Gorton—1987 national champion, 1999 senior world champion

Sponsors

Dunlop Sports

JLG Industries

Chenal Country Club

Momentus Golf

Oakley

Alltel Wireless

Excel Golf Tee

The Beast Energy Drink

Dillard's

Daniel Cremieux

Antigua Apparel

Acknowledgments

I had a lot of help turning my Long-Drive Bible into a book. Matt Rudy is a good friend, and I wouldn't trust anybody else to put words in my mouth. (He's also bigger than me, so I have to be careful what I say.) J. D. Cuban made me look better than I actually do in the pictures. Farley Chase is responsible for making this happen, and Stephen Power at Wiley did a great job editing the book. I also want to thank Guy Yocom at *Golf Digest*. He became an instant friend and was the first person to see the possibilities for my little black book.

I am very lucky to have some people in my life who never gave up on me and have been there for me no matter what.

There aren't enough words to describe how grateful I am to be my mother's son. Ann Mortimer raised seven of us on her own, and she's the driving force behind who I've become. I was a skinny kid, and she taught me not to ignore the negative comments people made about me but to use them as motivation to prove people wrong.

My brothers and sisters—Dan, Kevin, Corby, Victoria, Tami, Lisa, and Amanda—have all given me encouragement whenever I needed it. Vicki took out a personal loan to keep me at the University of Florida long enough to get the chance to earn a scholarship. She's always joking that I should say I owe everything to her, but she's absolutely right. She made some tremendous sacrifices for me.

Dan always stuck up for me, and he taught me some valuable lessons about dealing with people—ones he picked up as a drill sergeant in the marines. Here's a tip that's more valuable than any in this book: don't go pointing your finger in a drill sergeant's face when you get into an argument. I'm just lucky it was a left jab instead of a right hook, or I might still be asleep!

Tami is one of the only people I know who can consistently make me laugh. She's kept me light and focused, and it's been such a joy to watch her sons—my nephews—Tyler and Ben Hansbrough grow into great men and great basketball players.

Corby was my best man and still is. He's my fishing partner for life.

Lisa and I were born thirteen months apart, and she's always kept up with my accomplishments. She's been a great cheerleader for me throughout my life.

Because my father wasn't a part of my life, I've always looked for guidance from strong coaches. I've been very lucky to get some great ones. Back at Poplar Bluff High School, Bill Caputo laid down the law on me and kept me from going down some bad roads. He told me something I've never forgotten. I asked him why people were always teasing me. He said, "Fister, if these people didn't like you, they wouldn't say anything to you." I've always been proud of my ability to get along with just about anybody, and it's because Coach Caputo helped me realize that I shouldn't take myself too seriously. My other high school coach, Bill Cody, never stopped encouraging me.

Coach Mike Bozeman is one of the most impressive people I have ever met. A bona fide Vietnam War hero, Coach Bozeman was my field events coach at the University of Florida. He became a mentor to me the moment I met him, and I am a much better man for it. Integrity and honor are hallmarks of this man's character. Aside from my mother, he's the only person who always saw my potential to do great things. Coach Bozeman taught me to set my goals high and to have enough belief in myself to be relentless in my effort to accomplish them. I can't think of a better gift to give a twenty-year-old kid who didn't know his ass from his elbow.

John Daly deserves a thank-you for putting in a good word for me to people who were looking to hire for exhibitions. John's a great guy, and he's a great guy to have on your side. He's one of the most generous and caring people I have ever known. Most people see John as this everyday good ol' boy—and I've been out way past bedtime with him enough to know that that's part of who he is. But I've also seen the lengths he goes to for his friends, and more impressively, for terminally ill children. I've seen him get close to these kids and make their dreams come true, and I've seen him just wilt when one loses the battle. I love that about him more than anything.

The guys at Dunlop have been supporting my long-driving exploits for more than ten years, and the team I work with there is second to none—Neil Morton, Ahzim Kahn, and Bob Sameski. "Team Beast" also includes Chuck Peebles, Andy Troyan, Noel English, Chris Hellams, and Ashley Andrews. Guy Peters, David Vogrin, Chris Chappel, Tad Moore, Dan Murphy, and Shane Duffy deserve a lot of the credit as well going back through the years. Craig Paylor of JLG Industries is more than a sponsor; he's a friend and a mentor who is extremely competitive—and we both share that trait.

I've got a lot of terrific friends, but Tony Zadnick has been there longer than any of them. We've been best buddies since we were obnoxious seventh graders. Tony's parents, Tony and Carol, deserve medals for putting up with us—and I'll never forget how they treated me like one of their own.

Nobody has been a better or more unselfish friend than Randy Davidson. Along that same line, I want to thank Rocky Mantooth, Dan Hampton, Benny Holt, Chris Rushin, Doug Libla, Tommy Clarkson, Gene Hansbrough, the Doug (Hollings) Golf Association, Chris Goodwin and the staff at Red Tail Golf Club in Canada, and Buddy Godwin, who started me in long driving.

So many members at Chenal Country Club have given me great advice over the years that by naming any of them I'd be afraid I left somebody out. The entire membership has been so supportive. Our head pro, John Warburton, has smarts beyond his years, and those of us in the DGA will always call him the Best Pro in America.

"Big Steve" Strange is a loyal friend, and he lights up a room like nobody I've ever seen. He is a dedicated father, and his sons are lucky to have him. I really could have used him when I was growing up! Steve was also kind enough to arrange for us to shoot the photographs for this book at the beautiful Pauma Valley Country Club. The staff at the club is fantastic, and they went out of their way to help make these photos look great.

None of this would have been possible without my wife, Karen. She's my dream girl. I have loved her since I first laid eyes on her, and I practically stalked her until she let me take her out. I'm lucky she finally gave in and married me. She told me a few years after we were married that after our first date she went home and told her mother she had found the man she was going to marry. I sure as hell didn't know that, and she deserves an Oscar for that acting job. She played me perfect, though. She told me she knew that she was a challenge I would pursue, and she was right. I am a better man from sharing my life with such a wonderful person. My kids, Beau, Palmer, and Paige, are my whole world, and I am determined to give them a much better life than I had, and at the same time teach them the value of hard work and earning what you get, including respect from others.